UNLOCKING THE VAULT:

Keys to Manifesting God's Glory in Your Life

DAVID ALAN TAYLOR

DEDICATION

To my beautiful children whom I love: Presious, Shavonna, Dae'sha, Ryann, and Micah. I want you all to know that I love you very much. I thank God for you all being gifts unto me.

Table of Content

Acknowledgments

I want to acknowledge and honor a special, extraordinary, unique, wonderful, incredible, amazing lady in my life - Randryia Houston Taylor. I appreciate her patience, support, love, and dedication. My wife persistently encouraged me to finish this book. Her faith in me was consistent. To my wife - I love you, ladybug.

Introduction

First, I want to thank my Lord and Savior Jesus Christ and my precious friend, the Holy Spirit for inspiring me to write this book. For it was God that gave me the revelation concerning the glory of God. So, I honor God the Father as the true author of this book. This book is full of insightful mysteries and truths about the glory of God.

I shared powerful testimonies about divine visitations, spiritual dreams, and visions that I

1

have had. My heart is to reveal not a new revelation, but a revelation that was preserved and hid in God before the foundation of the world and now being revealed for such a time as this. These glory revelations will be confirmed by scripture.

I am excited for your journey in this book. I believe that you're going to be enlightened to understand the glory of God like never before. I trust that as you read this book, God grants you multiple impartations and visitations from the Lord.

Before you read this book, I want you to pray and ask God for a supernatural, glory visitation. The glory is greater than the realm of power, presence, anointing, and gifts. This book is going to reveal principles on how to experience the glory of God in your life in an awesome way.

CHAPTER 1

Glory Realm

I believe that we are living in a dispensation of time where God is getting ready to reveal his glory unto the body of Christ like we have never seen before. I am so excited about what God is getting ready to do on Earth. I'm talking about miracles, signs, wonders, and supernatural Glory manifestations, Hallelujah.

A true move of God starts within a hungry soul desperate for more of God and His presence. There must be a hunger in you to experience God in a way that supersedes any earthly ecstasy, crave, high, or desire. If this is you, I need you to open your heart to the Holy Spirit and allow His presence to lead you on a thrilling adventure into the depths of the glory of God.

Many years ago, the Lord spoke to me in a dream and He made me a promise. It is very possible for God to appear to you in a dream and speak with you (see 1 Kings 3:5). God said to me that my life shall be as a watered garden and I shall see the Glory of the Lord. At the time of the divine encounter, I didn't know that the term 'watered garden' meant in context of the Bible. One day, I was reading Isaiah 58:11 and I stumbled across the term - "And the Lord shall guide thee continually, and satisfy thy soul in drought, and make fat thy bones: and thou shalt be like a *watered garden*, and like a spring of water, whose waters fail not."

The Lord spoke these words to me as a promise that I would see His Glory. The day it happened, I didn't have the full meaning or interpretation of the dream. I just knew that I had experienced a divine encounter with God.

God is not prejudice or a respecter of person. He desires to visit you too, Hallelujah. As you begin to read this book, I want you to pray and ask God the Father to reveal more of Himself to you in a supernatural way. The word Glory in the Hebrew *kabowd* means weight, wealth, and abundance; which means that the Glory can come in many forms or manifestations.

Glory Weight

When we view glory from the perspective of weight, it shows that glory has the potential to crush, to compress, to defeat, to overpower, and to destroy. Any form of sin, demonic strongholds, or pre-planned attacks from the enemy will be supernaturally eradicated by the weight of the glory of God. The devil does not want you to be exposed to this revelation because he knows that if this key gets into the hands of a true, born again believer, that he and his demonic soldiers will not stand a chance against you.

According to 2 Chronicles 5:14, "So that the priest could not stand to minister by reason of the cloud; for the glory of the Lord had filled the house of God". The priests were not able to complete or carry out their duties because of the weight of the glory cloud. Exodus 40:35 says, "And Moses was not able to enter into the tent of congregation because of the weight God's glory.

Then, we see in Daniel 10:16 (NLT), "Then the one who looked like a man touched my lips, and I opened my mouth and began to speak. I said to the one standing in front of me, I am filled with anguish because of the vision I have seen, my Lord, and I am very weak." Daniel encountered the presence of the Lord, he became weak. As you can see there is weight to the glory.

Weight is defined as something heavy, an

overpowering force, or a strong influence. When the glory shows up, it comes as a heavy presence that overpowers anything that is demonic. The glory will bring pressure against the kingdom of darkness. Demonic systems, demonic powers, and demonic kingdoms will not stand a chance against the glory of God.

The glory is a strong influence; this means that it has power and authority to bring changing effect. I want to share a testimony of my glory experience. Some years ago, I experienced the weight of the Glory come upon on me in a powerful way. I was in my 20's when this visitation occurred. My then pastor was preparing to travel to Chicago, Illinois to preach at a church. So, the night before his preaching engagement, I went to the laundromat at about 12:00 am to wash some clothes to wear for the service.

As I was sitting in the laundromat, I began to feel a heavy presence. I thought that an angel, or maybe Jesus, had walked in due to the strong presence I felt. The presence began to grow stronger and stronger. My legs became very weak and I thought to myself, I don't want people to see me fall out in the middle of the floor. So, I attempted to run outside and get in my van. Right at the van door, I collapsed under the power of God.

I was arrested by the glory and began to weep before God. The location of the laundromat was on a busy street and many cars were driving by, but I just wept and embraced my God encounter. I remember that morning before the visitation, I had a feeling that something supernatural was going to happen. I was overpowered and under the influence of the glory. Sometimes, God allows us to have Supernatural encounters to receive divine impartation.

Heaven is full of glory, but God wants to bring that glory atmosphere to earth. Are you ready for it? If yes, then receive it by faith! It's your time to have a glory encounter!

My prayer: Lord release the weight of your glory upon every person that reads this book. I cannot take credit for the things I have written in this book because it was all given by the Holy Spirit who inspired me.

Glory Wealth

The glory can also come in the form of wealth. Remember, *kobowd* in the Hebrew means wealth. The glory is a supernatural manifestation of God, full of provisions, supplies, and resources that we need to fulfill purpose on Earth. The glory has power to produce supernatural wealth.

I call it *creative power*! As you learn how to operate in the glory realm, poverty will cease to exist in your life. The glory will bring supernatural blessing and prosperity to your life and household. Recall 2 Samuel 6:11, "And the ark of the Lord continued in the house of Obededom the Gittite three months: and the Lord blessed Obededom, and all his household."

As the ark of the Lord continued or inhabited, they remained blessed. The word 'continued' or the Hebrew word *Yashab* means inhabited, or lived in; so as long as the glory lives in your house, your household will be blessed. Now, there is a responsibility we must commit ourselves to in order to maintain the glory of God in our lives or household.

That responsibility or prerequisite is **sanctification.** Sanctification means to separate from the profane things and to dedicate ourselves to God. Profane things are unholy, ungodly, and sinful. There is a decision we as believers must make to experience this supernatural glory wealth.

We read in Philippians 4:19, "But my God shall supply all your needs according to His riches in glory in Christ Jesus." The word riches, in Greek *Ploutos,* means wealth, money, and abundance of external possessions. Apostle Paul reveals that riches, wealth, money, and abundance of external possessions is in the glory.

God desires for His children to go deeper in Him. There is another dimension that God wants to expose to you, but you must develop a lifestyle of self-discipline, self-sacrifice, self-control and self-restraint to be a partaker of this level of glory. In the earthly realm, principles are required such as the law of reciprocity to attain wealth, but in the glory realm, money will supernaturally manifest.

Glory Abundance

The glory also comes in the form of abundance. Abundance is defined as a plentiful amount of resources. All the resources we need on Earth are in the glory and I desire to give you the keys to unlock the door so that you can access your kingdom resources to complete your kingdom assignment on Earth.

It is in God's will to give you an abundance of wealth, joy, peace, happiness, strength, wisdom, miracles, knowledge, love, food supply, and the list goes on. When you operate in the system of glory, you will begin to experience a supernatural lifestyle of abundance and overflow. This is when you begin to experience the power of the kingdom of God on earth manifesting in your life to full capacity.

1 Kings 18:41 says, "And Elijah said unto Ahab, get thee up, and drink; for there is a sound of abundance of rain." The word abundance, or the Hebrew word *Hamown,* means wealth and riches. Abundance which symbolizes wealth and riches will come from the cloud according to verse 44, "And it came to pass at the seventh time, that he said Behold, there ariseth a little cloud out of the sea, like a man's hand. And he said, go up say unto Ahab, prepare thy chariot, and go get thee down, that the rain stop thee not."

Remember rain can also represent prosperity, abundance and blessings. Listen, beloved. It's now time to find the cloud of glory, access the cloud of glory, and extract with faith, giving, prayer, worship, and fasting your resources, supply, and provisions!

Glory System

Many times, we as Christians hear the term 'Glory Realm'. My question is, do we really know what this term means or do we use this term out of cliché? Let me first define the meaning of the word *realm* which means kingdom, sphere, environment, or level. The word kingdom can mean order, and order is a system. This implies that there's a system to the glory. Many have tried to access the glory through carnal, religious, legalistic, dogmatic, secular, self-righteous, and false denominational systems.

Romans 10:3 says, "For they being ignorant of God's righteousness, and going about to establish their own righteousness, have not submitted themselves unto the righteousness of God." Once we have learned and mastered the glory system, we then can access that realm with glory manifestations following.

There are principles and rules to the glory system. Many in the body of Christ have deviated from the glory system, and as a result, they are not experiencing the Glory manifestations. We must rediscover the ancient Glory system to regain access to this realm. Psalm 25:14 states, "The secret of the LORD is with them that fear him; and he will shew them his covenant". The ISV version says, "The intimate counsel of the LORD is for those who fear him so they may know his covenant".

As you begin to position yourself to understand the glory system as a son and a friend to God, with a heart of reverence, the Father of Glory is going to begin to share intimate counsel with you.

Reverence is rule #1. Reverence is key to unlocking and accessing the secrets of God. Reverence is worship performed to show respect and honor.

Rule #2 is fasting, Exodus 33:18," And he said, I beseech thee, shew me thy glory". Moses had been fasting for 40 days and that positioned him to ask God to show him the glory. Fasting also *qualified* him for a glory experience. Fasting means to abstain from food for spiritual purpose and is one of the greatest key for supernatural breakthrough.

Isaiah 58:8 says, "Then shall thy light break forth as the morning, and thine health shall spring forth speedily; and thy righteousness shall go before thee; the Glory of the Lord shall be thy reward." The NLT says, "That the Lord shall protect you from behind."

Before the Israelites crossed through the Red Sea and onto dry land, according to Exodus 14:19, "And the angel of God, which went before the camp of Israel, removed and went behind them; and the pillar of the cloud went from before their face, and stood behind them." When you fast, the glory will be your reward. The glory will go before you and the glory will protect you from behind. As you discipline yourself to live a lifestyle of fasting, you will experience a lifestyle of glory manifestations.

Rule #3 is worship. Worship is when we acknowledge the worth and value of God. Worship is when your heart and the Father's heart become one, which creates an intimate bond and oneness between you and Him. Worship is the sacrifice of oneself.

Recall Genesis 22:5, "And Abraham said unto his young men, Abide ye here with the ass; and I and the lad will go yonder and worship, and come again to you." If you notice, on mount Moriah, Abraham did not display worship in the form of prostration because his worship was displayed in the form of sacrifice in his attempt in sacrificing Isaac. True worship is sacrifice of oneself.

Rule #4 is spiritual hunger. Fasting will create a supernatural hunger in you for more of God and His presence. When there is a spiritual hunger in you, God will release heavenly things unto you. We read in Nehemiah 9:15, "And gavest them bread from heaven for their hunger, and broughtest forth water for them out of the rock for their thirst, and promisedst them that they should go in to possess the land which thou hadst sworn to give them."

As you begin to understand the glory system rules, your life will become extraordinary, uncommon, and supernatural. Exodus 25:40, "And look that thou make them after their pattern, which was shewed thee in the mount." God revealed the heavenly pattern of the tabernacle and its furniture unto Moses. A pattern is a blueprint, method, paradigm, and system. As you can see, God gave Moses the system, or method of rules, so that he could approach the presence of God correctly. Moses did not deviate from this system.

Here the Bible says that King David set the ark upon a new cart. God's original plan for the ark of the covenant was for it to be carried upon the shoulders of the Levites (see 1 Chronicles 15:15). This means that God wants His children to carry His presence, not a new cart carrying His presence. A new cart way can represent man's way. God isn't interested in man's way, it has to be His way. To discover God's way is to discover God's system. The glory of God will follow God's system and not man's system. King David made a mistake when he changed the system by placed the ark of the covenant on a new cart (see 2 Samuel 6:3). Like David, many Christians have deviated from the Glory System.

Glory Sphere

Then next definition for realm is sphere, which means a field for activity or operation. The glory works best in a celestial atmosphere created by worship. A celestial sphere is a supernatural, heavenly, divine, angelic, transcendent environment.

So, as we begin to engage in pure worship, the atmosphere shifts into a glory sphere just like the place of Eden where Adam lived. Pure worship is important because it deals with the heart, attitude, and character of a person that is trying to create a place for God to inhabit. We read in Matthew 5:8, "Blessed are the pure in heart: for they will see God." As you can see, the heart must be pure, clean, blameless, and free from corrupt desires. A pure heart will create pure worship and pure worship will create a celestial glory sphere. Worship is the highest form of prayer and the highest level of ecstasy. There is a synergy that worship brings when connected to a pure heart. I call it **"Glory Power"**.

Recall Ephesians 2:2, "Wherein in time past ye walked according to the course of this world, according to the prince of the power of the air, the spirit that now worketh in the children of disobedience." The prince is Satan, who has authority over the atmospheric realm. When worship is being practiced, demonic activities that control and rule that sphere will be broken. That sphere will then become a glory sphere which as stated before is a celestial, supernatural, heavenly, divine, angelic, transcendent environment.

Glory Environment

The word realm is also defined as environment. An environment is the area in which something exists or lives. There is a place called the Garden of Eden where Adam lived. Genesis 2:8 "And the Lord planted a garden eastward in Eden; and there he put the man whom he had formed." The Garden of Eden was Adam's Glory Environment.

The Garden of Eden was a place where God and Adam were cohabiting together. God desires for you to have a glory environment so that He can cohabitate with you too. When you create a glory environment by fasting, worship, consecration and intimate fellowship with God (the Father, the Son, and the Holy Spirit), you then will experience peace, pleasure, power, presence, and provision in your Eden.

Your environment determines the life you shall have. If your environment is confusion, your life will be confusion. If your environment is dysfunctional, your life will be dysfunctional. If your environment is peace, you will live a life of peace and tranquility. If your environment is worship, you will live a life of power, presence, and glory. Your life and reality reflects your environment.

Glory Dimensions
The word dimension means measurement in length, width, depth, and height. There are many dimensions to the glory of God. In Paul the Apostle teachings to the Corinthian church, he states, "from glory to glory," which implies that there are many dimensions, realms, degrees and levels of glory (See 2 Corinthians 3:18).

This chapter is going to help you understand the Glory in its different facets. Many use the terms *dimension* and *level* interchangeably, but there is a difference. Let me define the word *level.* Levels in a plural sense is a series of stages. There are so many levels and dimensions to the glory that many have not experienced. Many Christians have not experienced new levels and dimensions of the glory because they have become so complacent in their walk with God. This is why fasting is important because it creates a supernatural hunger in the believer for more of God. It is that supernatural hunger that gives us the desire and drive to seek after greater levels, dimensions, and realms of glory.

The average Christian has become distracted by the cares of this world. Social media, reality TV shows, and cell phones contribute to carnality in the Christian lifestyle. Jeremiah 6:16, "Thus saith the Lord; stand ye in the ways, and see, and ask for the old paths, where is the good way, and walk therein, and ye shall find rest for your souls. But they said, we will not walk therein."

The old path is the path of righteousness. This path will lead us to God, prepare us for multiple glory encounters, depending on our level of seeking and hunger for God. The glory of God is multi-dimensional as we see in 2 Corinthians 3:18, "But we all, with open face beholding as in a glass the glory of the Lord, are changed into the same image from Glory to Glory, even as by the spirit of the Lord."

If you desire this ever-increasing glory, you must seek, search, look for, pursue, crave, strive, and invoke God for more of his glory. We read in Haggai 2:9, "The Glory of this latter house shall be greater than of the former, saith the Lord of host: and in the place will I give peace, saith the Lord of Hosts."

This word *greater*, the Hebrew *Gadowl,* means mighty, high, larger, deeper, heavy, exceedingly, intensity. So, if prophecy reveals that there will be a greater glory there must be a lesser glory. 1 Corinthians 15:41, "There is one Glory of the sun, and another Glory of the moon, and another Glory of the stars: for one star different from another star in Glory." Remember glory can come in many forms. The sun has glory, the moon has glory, the stars have glory, but each glory is different.

I mentioned earlier in this chapter that glory can come in the form of weight, wealth, and abundance, glory can come in many more forms. I only mention a few. I believe as you continue to read this book, the inner witness, the Holy Spirit, is going to begin to stimulate a greater level of hunger within you for a mightier, heavier, and stronger glory experience. I want you to take a pause now and tell the Father of Glory (God), **I WANT MORE OF YOUR GLORY.**

Glory Knowledge

Many in the body of Christ lack the ability to enter, shift or even carry the glory simply because many don't really understand what the glory is and its purpose. Some may have a basic or surface level knowledge of the glory, while others may have a false, preconceived idea of the glory. There is a mystery concerning the glory that God wants us to seek out.

Proverbs 25:2 offers, "It is the Glory of God to conceal a thing: but the honor of kings to search out the matter." It is God's glory to conceal a thing. The word conceal comes from the Hebrew word *cathar* which means to hide by covering. According to Revelations 1:6, "And hath made us kings and priests unto God and his father; to Him be glory and dominion forever and ever. Amen." So as kings, it is our honor to search out the matter, the things that God has concealed. The key to the glory is in our seeking and searching as kings in the earth.

The scripture also identifies a woman as king. In the natural, a woman married to a king was given the title as a queen. Spiritually, God looks upon women as a king not just men, giving them power to operate in authority and power too. Many believers have become lazy in their study and pursuit to learn more about the Father of Glory.

Every day, we ought to be educating ourselves about the things of God. I encourage you to educate, dig deep, and study as much as you can concerning the Glory of God. I personally believe that your life will never be the same again. As you study the glory, I believe that a glory portal will begin to open and out of that portal will be released unto you glory revelation.

What you study determines the realm you access. If you study love, the realm of love will be open unto you. If you study prosperity, the realm of prosperity will be open unto you. If you study glory, the realm of glory will be open unto you. Now there is a prerequisite and that is faith and action.

Once glory revelation has been given unto you, there must be application on your part for these realms to be activated. Application means a diligent effort. I take authority over the spirit of laziness, idleness, and procrastination and I decree and declare over you diligent engagement, glory effortful engagement, prayerful engagement and studious engagement in Jesus mighty name.

Personal study and devotion must be a priority in your life. Fill your mind with the knowledge of the Glory of God. Begin to study scriptures about the glory and the Holy Spirit which is the spirit of Glory will begin to reveal or make known the deeper meaning of the Glory of God unto you. It is God's will for the earth to be filled with the knowledge of his Glory. Habakkuk 2:14 says, "For the earth shall be filled with the knowledge of the Glory of the LORD, as the waters cover the sea."

Knowledge is the key to access. If you fill your mind with the knowledge of the glory, you then can access the glory. Remember the scripture said the wise, meaning the learned, shall inherit glory. Knowledge is information that shows us how to access, operate, and shift the glory.

Access means to have permission to enter. Our Lord and Savior Jesus Christ was the key of access to the knowledge of the Glory of God 2 Corinthians 4:6, "For God, who commanded the light to shine out of darkness, hath shined in our hearts, to give the light of the knowledge of the glory of God in the face of Jesus Christ".

The word *face*, in the Greek *prosopon,* means person or presence. So, as we spend quality time in the presence of Jesus Christ, the knowledge of the glory of God is revealed in our hearts. Worship, prayer, and devotion are intimate tools that will strengthen our relationship with Christ, and then will God the Father, and the Holy Spirit begin to shine in our hearts the light of the knowledge of the Glory of God that's revealed in the face or presence of Jesus Christ.

Seeing the Glory

Does God want to reveal His glory to you?
Absolutely! Psalm 97:6 states, "The heavens
declare his righteousness, and all the people
see his Glory". The glory is something that
God desires for you to see. Many believe we
are not supposed to see the glory of God as
they lean to Isaiah 42:8, "I am the LORD:
that is my name: and my Glory will I not give
to another, neither my praise to graven
images". They use this scripture to justify
their argument, but that word glory in this
verse means honor.

God was saying my honor will I give to no
other, for there is an honor that only belongs
to God. The scripture teaches us in Proverbs
3:35, "The wise shall inherit Glory: but
shame shall be the promotion of fools." As a
Kingdom citizen, the glory belongs to you by
inheritance. The wise, skillful, prudent, and
the learned shall inherit glory. The word
inherit, or the Hebrew word *nashal,* means to
take possession of and to receive with the
ability to control.

We can control what we possess. If you possess a car, you have the power to control that car. If you possess a bus, you have power to control that bus. If you possess plane, you have the power to control plane. If you possess the glory, you have the ability and power to control glory as a glory carrier.

Control means to manage, oversee, and guide. In the Old Testament, the Levitical priests managed, oversaw, and guided the Ark of the Covenant which represented the Glory of God. We read in 1 Chronicles 15:2, "Then David said, None ought to carry the ark of God but the Levites: for them hath the Lord chosen to carry the ark of God, and to minister unto him forever". We too as believers have that privilege and honor to manage, oversee, and guide the presence and Glory of God.

When Stephen was being stoned he saw the glory. Acts 7:55 says, "But he, being full of the Holy Ghost, looked up steadfastly into heaven, and saw the Glory of God, and Jesus standing on the right hand of God..." Like Stephen, God allows us to go through persecution to prepare us for a glory experience. There is always persecution before there is glory. Trials are prophetic confirmation that glory is about to show up in your life.

When Jesus took Peter, James, and John on Mount Transfiguration they saw the glory. Luke 9:32 says, "and when they were awake, they saw his Glory, and the two men that stood with him." The church will never see the Glory of God until the church has been awakened. Paul the Apostle of Jesus Christ writes in Ephesians 5:14, "Wherefore he saith, Awake thou that sleepest, and arise from the dead, and Christ shall give thee light".

God's heart and pleasure is to see the church, his bride, awakened to glory revelation. Once we allow the Father of Glory to awaken us, we then will see the Glory of God. In the case of Martha, belief was required for her to witness the Glory of God (see John 11:40). These three scriptures reveal three things required to see the Glory of God. With Stephen it was persecution, with Peter, James, and John they were awakened, and with Martha belief was the prerequisite. **Persecution, being awakened, and belief** are the three keys to seeing the glory.

CHAPTER 2

Lifestyle of Consecration

As a Priest we are called to live a lifestyle of consecration. It becomes very difficult to practice the presence of God when your life isn't consecrated. *Consecration*, or the Hebrew word *qadash,* means holy, or to sanctify, to purify and to set apart for the work of God. Consecration is to be devoted to a sacred duty. Aaron and his sons were consecrated to serve as priests according to Exodus 30:30, "And thou shalt anoint Aaron and his sons, and consecrate them, that they may minister unto me in the priest's office."

Consecration is a key that will prepare you to walk in supernatural power and once you practice this principle key the presence of God will empower your life and ministry. Consecration will unlock spiritual realms for supernatural intervention and intensify the miraculous in your life.

Everyone who wants to be a prophet, apostle, evangelist, pastor, or teacher in the Lord's church is first called into the office of the priest. The priest's office is often overlooked and avoided due to the requirements for holy living. The power of God is not available to any vessel that is not willing to live their lives consecrated before the Lord. The Old Testament priest lived a lifestyle of consecration.

The priests could not serve in the temple until the age of thirty. We read in 1 Chronicles 23:2-5, "And he gathered together all the princes of Israel, with the priests and the Levites. Now the Levites were numbered from the age of thirty years and upward: and their number by their polls, man by man, was thirty and eight thousand. Of which, twenty and four thousand were to set forward the work of the house of the Lord; and six thousand were officers and judges: Moreover, four thousand were porters; and four thousand praised the Lord with the instruments which I made, said David, to praise therewith." I want you to remember that the number thirty is the number of consecration and maturity for ministry.

Joseph did not become second man in command or prime minister over Egypt until he was thirty years old per Genesis 41:46, "And Joseph was thirty years old when he stood before Pharaoh King of Egypt. And Joseph went out from the presence of Pharaoh, and went throughout all the land of Egypt." David does not begin his reign over Israel until he was thirty years old as seen in 2 Samuel 5:4, "David was thirty years old when he began to reign, and he reigned forty years." Jesus did not begin his public ministry until he was thirty years old as we read in Luke 3:23, "And Jesus himself began to be about thirty years of age, being (as was supposed) the son of Joseph, which was the son of Heli..." So, the number thirty is a very significant number that represents consecration and maturity for ministry.

We must embrace the spirit of consecration because without consecration, there will be a void in your life and that void will be the presence of God. Whatever the Lord have called you to do, it is consecration that will supernaturally invoke the hand of God to invade your life causing you to fulfill that mission effectively. I am not saying that you are not going to go through warfare and tough times in your life, but what consecration does is position you to experience the release of the presence of God upon you, by way of divine intervention (angels, anointings, and presence) to undergird you, pushing you into purpose and power.

Consecration gives us an advantage and supernatural leverage in life. In the Book of Exodus 30:30, God speaks to Moses and says, "And thou shalt anoint Aaron and his sons, and consecrate them, that they may minister unto me in the priest's office". So again, consecration is something that we are called to embrace.

One thing about the great leaders of the faith like Smith Wigglesworth, A.A. Allen, Charles Finney, Father Nash, John Wesley, Katherine Kuhlman, the reason why their ministries were supernaturally empowered, was because they understood the principle of consecration. The Lord spoke to me some years ago and said these words to me "preaching without prayer is powerless motivation". In the same way, preaching without consecration is powerless motivation.

This is why God desires to restore consecration back to the Body of Christ. And

I believe once we begin to see the spirit of consecration return to the church we will see signs, wonders, and miracles. The priests were not allowed to carry the Ark of the Covenant if they were not consecrated. We read in 1 Chronicles 15:14, "So the priests and the Levites sanctified themselves to bring up the ark of the Lord God of Israel".

Only the consecrated will walk in power, operate in the supernatural, and raise the dead. The Bible teaches us that the priests were authorized to eat the table of shewbread which was consecrated bread every Sabbath. 1 Samuel 21:6 NIV states, "So the priest gave him the consecrated bread, since there was no bread there except the bread of the Presence that had been removed from before the Lord and replaced by hot bread on the day it was taken away." Shewbread was also called the bread of presence. The bread remained in the presence of God for seven days, and on the seventh day, the priests were allowed to eat the consecrated bread.

In your consecration you have no business allowing your spirit to eat sinful things such as: gossip, fornication, pride, witchcraft, idolatry, blasphemy, profanity, and rebellion, disobedience to authority, hatred, strife, envy, drunkenness, extortion, unforgiveness and evil thoughts. Eating these things can be very unhealthy to your spiritual development and character. The word sanctify means to separate from the profane things and to be dedicated to God.

So, ask yourself the question, what have I been eating? Remember, we are what we eat. We ought to be eating prayer, worship, the word of God, and consecration so that we become transformed into the image of God.

Priestly Anointing

Recall Revelation 1:6, "And hath made us kings and priests unto God and his Father; to him be glory and dominion for ever and ever. Amen." The Bible clearly states that God has made you both kings and priests. I believe that Revelation 1:6 is revealing the ministry of Melchizedek. The Melchizedek ministry establishes us as both kings and priests in the kingdom of God. This two-fold anointing and ministry has been given to you by spiritual adoption Romans 8:15, "For ye have not received the spirit of bondage again to fear; but ye have received the Spirit of adoption, whereby we cry, Abba, Father."

Adoption means to place as a son. So, through sonship, this kingly anointing and priestly anointing belongs to you by birthright. King David prophesied that Jesus would be a priest after the order of Melchizedek in Psalm 110:4, "The Lord hath sworn, and will not repent, Thou art a priest for ever after the order of Melchizedek." This is also found in the New Testament, Hebrews 6:20, "Whither the forerunner is for us entered, even Jesus, made a high priest forever after the order of Melchisedec."

According to Hebrews 8:6, "But now hath he obtained a more excellent ministry, by how much also he is the mediator of a better covenant, which was established upon better promises." Jesus obtained a more superior ministry and that ministry was the Melchizedek order. Read Genesis Chapter 14 for more details about the character and life of Melchizedek.

In the Old Testament, the word priest comes from a Hebrew word *kohen* which means a chief ruler. The priests perform ritualistic, sacrificial, and mediatorial duties. The word kohen comes from a root word in the Hebrew Kahan which simply means to mediate.

So, the priest served in the Old Testament as mediators. That's why I love to tell people that the prophets represented God before the people but the priest represented the people before God. For the Bible declares in 1 Peter 2:9, "But ye are a chosen generation, a royal priesthood, an holy nation, a peculiar people; that ye should shew forth the praises of him who hath called you out of darkness into his marvelous light..." For God has called us as a chosen generation, a royal priesthood, a holy nation.

Therefore, in New Testament scripture, God has called us to be priests. We're no longer priests after the Levitical order but we're priests after the order of Melchizedek. Hebrews 7:12, "For the priesthood being changed, there is made of necessity a change also of the law." As New Testament believers, we have shifted from the Levitical order to the order of Melchizedek.

Adam's Priestly Anointing
In Genesis we find that Adam's priestly anointing was found in his worship. Genesis 2:15 offers, "And the Lord God took the man and put him into the Garden of Eden to dress it and to keep it." The word *dressed*, or the Hebrew word *abad*, means to work, serve and worship. Worship is a priestly anointing.

So, Adam from the beginning was walking in this priestly anointing and in this priestly anointing he gains access to the presence of God. So now, he's greeted by hearing the voice of God every day in Eden. When Adam disobeyed God, the voice of God came to the man and said, "Adam where art thou?" Not that God did not know where Adam was because God is omniscience which means that God is all knowing. Adam was no longer found in his priestly place, the place of intimacy.

It was God's intention to be in partnership, fellowship, and communion with man. So, when Adam messed up, the Bible says that Adam and Eve had hid themselves from the presence of God. Before they hid themselves, they lived, dwelled, and abided in the presence of God.

The word *presence*, or the Hebrew word *paniym* means face; which means that every day, Adam was having a face-to-face encounter with God. Consecration will prepare you to have a face to face encounter with God. The Bible said in Genesis 32:30,

"And Jacob called the name of the place Peniel: for I have seen God face to face, and my life is preserved." *Peniel* means 'for I have seen God face to face and my life is preserved'. God will preserve you in His presence!

The Ephod
In the Old Testament, we look at the high priest who wore a garment called an Ephod. The word Ephod in Hebrew means image. Why does it mean image? It means image because when God looked upon man, He was able to recognize the image of Himself in man.

The question is, when God sees you does He see Himself? Does He see carnality or does He recognize Himself in you? Jesus said, "When you see me, you see the Father. When God sees you, can he see himself in you? In order for the priest to be entrusted to wear the Ephod, his life had to be consecrated. If his life wasn't consecrated and holy, God wouldn't have permitted him to wear the Holy Ephod.

At the bottom of the Ephod were gold bells that wound release a sound as they would walk. There's a certain sound as consecrated priest we ought to carry. If God did not hear that sound of the gold belles the priest would die. What sound are you producing?

You would never be able to produce the sound of the Kingdom if your life isn't consecrated. The sound becomes distorted when you're producing the sound from an unholy place. Those who are in tune with the spirit of the Lord can discern that there's something wrong with the sound that's being produced from an unholy place or unholy vessels.

Our goal should be to get back to the sound of righteousness, holiness, and kingdom. God heard a sound coming from gold bell at the bottom of the high priest garment of the Ephod. God is still looking for that sound in our worship. He is still looking for that sound in our praise. He is still looking for that sound in our Thanksgiving. What sound does God hear from you - is it the sound of doubt, mediocrity, failure, or defeat? What sound are you producing? Is it the sound of success, greatness, love, or Kingdom?

God created man in Genesis 1:26 after his image and likeness. The word likeness by definition means echo, and an echo is a repeated sound. It is not our responsibility to *change* the sound it is our responsibility to *be the echo* of that sound. So, what sound are you echoing? In order to get back to the original sound, we must go back to consecration.

At the bottom of the garment there were also pomegranates. Pomegranates were fruits, meaning not only did the priest walk in a certain sound, but as priests, we are to walk in the fruit of the spirit. Galatians 5:22 elaborates, "But the fruit of the Spirit is love, joy, peace, longsuffering, gentleness, goodness, faith."

These are the nine fruits of the Spirit. What fruits are you producing? Not only does God wants us to carry a sound, but God is also looking for fruit to be produced in your life. The greatest way for you to produce love, joy, longsuffering, peace, and meekness is by living a consecrated lifestyle.

On the breastplate of the high priest, there were two stones called the Urim and the Thummim. Urim meaning life, Thummim meaning the light of perfection. These two stones gave the high priest revelation by God.

If you want to take on the spirit of wisdom and revelation upon your life, begin to consecrate yourself. There are some things that will never be revealed to you until you consecrate yourself before the Lord. The Bible said that the secrets of the Lord are with them that fear him. The word *secret*, or the Hebrew word *sad*, means confidential talk, private plans, and secret councils (Psalms 25:14).

When you begin to get intimate with God in consecration, prayer, and fasting, God then begins to share these revelations with you. Can God trust you with revelation? Revelation is only for the seekers and those that have decided to discipline themselves in consecration. Consecration is not an event, consecration ought to be a lifestyle.

Priestly Duties

The priest's responsibility was to watch over the fire on the altar of burnt offerings and to keep the fire burning both day and night. According to Leviticus 6:12, "And the fire upon the altar shall be burning in it; it shall not be put out: and the priest shall burn wood on it every morning, and lay the burnt offering in order upon it; and he shall burn thereon the fat of the peace offerings." And in 2 Chronicles 13:11, we read, "And they burn unto the Lord every morning and every evening burnt sacrifices and sweet incense: the shewbread also set they in order upon the pure table; and the candlestick of gold with the lamps thereof, to burn every evening: for we keep the charge of the Lord our God; but ye have forsaken him".

God has called you as a priestly watchman with the responsibility to start glory fires and to keep the glory fires from burning out. The purpose for glory fire is to consume everything that is not like God. Many people are bound by sins and curses they desire to be liberated from, but when there's no glory fire, they remain bound by the enemy. The enemy's strategy to keep the glory fire from burning is to keep those that are called to be priestly, holy, and consecrated, carnal and prayerless.

When we view the position of ushers in the church, our understanding of them is that they only go around the sanctuary with tissue in their hand, collecting gum from those who have been caught chewing in church. I'm not saying that this is something they shouldn't do, I'm just saying that there is more to their responsibility and function. Ushers are the modern day priestly watchmen and gatekeepers. They should be watching for the enemy, guarding the doors of the sanctuary, and interceding against any opposing spirit and force.

Every usher should be trained in the ministry of prayer and intercession and trained as priestly gatekeepers at the door on how to guard the house of God and His presence. We see in 1 Chronicles 9:26-27 NLT, "The four chief gatekeepers, all Levites, were trusted officials, for they were responsible for the rooms and treasuries at the house of God. They would spend the night around the house of God, since it was their duty to guard it and to open the gates every morning."

The job of the priest was not only to watch over the fire, but also to keep the fire burning. It's one thing to start a glory fire, but it is another thing to keep glory fire burning. I don't just want to see revival break out, I desire to see revival continue burning as a forest fire. Revival usually ends when the saints begin to lose their hunger and passion for God. Prayer meetings begin to dwindle, we go from great numbers to small numbers in attendance. The enemy then tricks us to go back to the norm.

It is time to get our fire back. We that are believers are supposed to be a flame of fire according to Hebrews 1:7, "And of the angels he saith, Who maketh his angels spirits, and his ministers a flame of fire." I encourage you to be a revivalist to your generation and ignite glory fires in your churches, schools, hospitals, prisons, bars, houses, cities, states and nations. Glory fires starts with prayer and fasting. Ask God the Father to release the spirit of prayer upon you and to give you a supernatural hunger for more of him. Ask the Father to give you the grace to fast and to pray longer hours.

Disconnect yourself from everything that serves as a distraction. Sacrifice your pleasures and seek for more of his presence. Continue this until you feel the weight of his presence becoming stronger upon you. Do this every day until you break through to God.

Ask God to give you the heart of an evangelist and to teach you how to be a revivalist. As a priest, it's time for you to be a starter of glory fires like we see in Hosea 10:12, "Sow to yourselves in righteousness, reap in mercy; break up your fallow ground: for it is time to seek the Lord, till he come and rain righteousness upon you." **IT'S TIME TO SEEK THE LORD!**

Lamp with No Oil

The priests were also responsible to feed the lamps with oil (see Exodus 27:20-21 and Leviticus 24:2). The word *pure,* or the Hebrew word *zak,* means clean and righteous. The oil would not continue burning all night if the oil wasn't clean. If the oil was contaminated, the fire would burn out. As a priest, to keep the fire burning, you must make sure that you are producing pure oil from a pure place. As a priest, your life must be clean and righteous, Psalm 132:9, "Let thy priests be clothed with righteousness; and let thy saints shout for joy."

If you're witnessing the fire of God ceasing to burn continuously in your life, it might be that there is some sin in your life that you refuse to acknowledge. In my past, I too have avoided acknowledging certain sins due to the pleasure, excitement, and gratification these sins brought to my flesh. The reason why I am being transparent with you about my past sins is because I don't want you to feel as if I am judging you.

The truth I must declare to you is that as many sins God has delivered me from, I know God is able to deliver you too, glory to God! I'm here as a friend and a brother to encourage you in your process. The oil represents the anointing of the Holy Ghost. There is an anointing that God desires to place upon you, but again, you must make sure your life is free from demonic activities to produce a powerful, lasting anointing. As the priest fed the lamps with oil, you too are called to feed your generation the oil of wisdom, oil of power, oil of love, oil of unity, and the oil of glory.

Oil Running Low

In many of our churches, the oil meaning the anointing is beginning to run low. As priests, it is our job to make sure that the House of God is replenished with the oil of His presence. During the time of Eli, the high priest, the oil was running low in the lamp in the temple of God 1 Samuel 3:3, "And ere the lamp of God went out in the temple of the Lord, where the ark of God was, and Samuel was laid down to sleep." This indicates that the priests were being slowful and not being diligent in their responsibility in keeping the lamp replenished with oil.

There is no oil in many of our churches because many of our leaders are not consecrating themselves to produce the oil that the sick, the broken, the afflicted, the confused, the cursed, the depressed, and the lost need. If there's no oil, there's no fire, if there's no fire, there's no light. The oil represents the anointing of the Holy Spirit and the fire is the consuming presence of the Holy Spirit. The light represents the revelation of God that's given to us by the Holy Spirit, which is the spirit of wisdom and revelation according to Ephesians 1:17, "That the God of our Lord Jesus Christ, the Father of glory, may give unto you the spirit of wisdom and revelation in the knowledge of him."

Now that we know that in the New Testament the oil represents the Holy Spirit, it takes the anointing of the Holy Spirit to break every yoke and to dismantle demonic powers and curses that were inherited through sins. It is so imperative to get back to the place of communing with the Holy Spirit like in 2 Corinthians 13:14, "The grace of the Lord Jesus Christ, and the love of God, and the communion of the Holy Ghost, be with you all. Amen."

The word *communion,* or the Greek *konini,*
means fellowship, intercourse, intimacy,
communication, partnership and sharing.
The Holy Spirit wants to fellowship with you,
communicate with you, be in partnership
with you and share intimate things with you.

The Holy Spirit is looking for lamps,
figuratively speaking; people that He can
dwell in and use. In the scripture, King David
was identified as a lamp in Psalm 132:17,
"There will I make the horn of David to bud:
I have ordained a lamp for mine anointed."
According to the scripture, your spirit is a
lamp as we see in Proverbs 20:27, "The spirit
of man is the candle of the Lord, searching
all the inward parts of the belly."

Morning and Evening Sacrifice
The priest's duty was also to offer morning
and evening sacrifice (see Exodus 29: 38-44).
That means that every day, the priests were
sacrificing something. My question to you is
what are you sacrificing? I, too, am not

exempt from this question.

As a priestly leader, I need to be sacrificing something daily as well. The priest offered two lambs, one in the morning and one in the evening. The lamb is a type of Christ. As a priest, we ought to be offering Jesus Christ to someone every day. To offer Christ Jesus is to offer His love and plan of salvation. The reason why sacrifice is so important, is because if there's no sacrifice, God will not send a fire. **No sacrifice, no fire.**

Priests Teach Laws of God

As a priest your duty is also to teach the laws of God as we read in 2 Chronicles 15:3, "Now for a long season Israel hath been without the true God, and without a teaching priest, and without law." The scriptures revealed that there was a time in Israel when there were no teaching priests. Whether you are a male or female, in the spirit, God sees you as a priest. And as a priest, your assignment is to teach and preach God's laws, which is the word of God to the world.

Being a priest is more than just living a lifestyle of consecration God wants us also to be filled with the word of God. We have been commissioned not only as carriers of the Word, but also as teachers of the Word as we read in Mark 16:15, "And He said unto them, Go ye into all the world, and preach the gospel to every creature." I feel afraid for innocent believers that are connected to those who have titles, but have no Word in them. How can you teach, lead God's people, or even defeat the devil if you're not studied in the scriptures?

The Bible speaks about prophets not having the Word in them in Jeremiah 5:13, "And the prophets shall become wind, and the word is not in them: thus shall it be done unto them." As priests, it's our job to establish the doctrine of Jesus Christ in our churches, homes, schools, and even in the prisons. You will not survive as a victorious priest if you have not God's Word in your heart.

I see so many priests today that are so unlearned in the scriptures. It is our responsibility to properly rightly divide the Word of truth. You must be a Holy Spirit filled priest to accurately discern, interpret, and translate the scriptures. You will self-destruct and break under the pressures of this chaotic and confused world if your life and mind is void of the Word of God.

Choose to be skilled in the Word. The Word is your power, your weapon. It is a book full of kingdom strategies and kingdom constitution against the devil and his kingdom. Many in the body of Christ are being destroyed because of the lack of knowledge according to Hosea 4:6 NIV, "Because you have rejected knowledge, I also reject you as my priests; because you have ignored the law of your God, I also will ignore your children."

The word *destroy*, or the Hebrew word *damah,* means to perish and to cut off. Many have been cut off from the kingdom simply because they lack having the Word of God which connects us to the kingdom of God. The kingdom of God is moved by the word. In Hosea 4:6 NIV, God spoke about the priests lacking God's knowledge and rejecting God's knowledge. As a result, God said that he would reject the priests for ignoring his laws. I encourage you to pick up your Bible and educate yourself in the scriptures. For God is looking for teaching priests that He can use to teach His word.

One of the prerequisites for being a qualified priest, according to the Old Testament, was that he was to be studied in the laws of God. Remember you are a priest before you are an apostle, prophet, evangelist, pastor, teacher, bishop, elder or deacon. If you are not called to any of these offices, there is one office that God has called us all to and that is the office of the priest.

God is looking for 5-fold priests, meaning apostolic priest, prophetic priest, evangelistic priest, pastoral priest and teaching priests. God is also looking for clergy priests meaning bishop priests, elder priests, and deacon priests that are apt to administering the Word of God. The apostles were apostolic priests and they continued steadfastly in the apostle's doctrine according to Acts 2:42, "And they continued steadfastly in the apostles' doctrine and fellowship, and in breaking of bread, and in prayers."

The clergy is made up of people that have been trained and approved for religious service. The word clergy comes from two old French words which mean 'learned men's. Clergy also come from the Latin word *clericatus* which means office of the priest. So as a priest, you ought to be learned in the scripture, trained for ministry and approved by God to carry out the mission He has called you too.

CHAPTER 3

Worship is the Access Key to Glory

Worship can come in many forms. Worship can come in the form of singing, giving, bowing, serving, and character. Worship comes from an old English word *worth-ship* which means to acknowledge the worth or value of something. True worship is when we acknowledge the worth and value of God.

It's when we value the worth of His presence, the worth of His love, and the worth of His sacrifice on Calvary's cross. Worship is when everything about God becomes more valuable to you than anything else. The Hebrew word for worship *kabowd,* means to bow down or prostrate. In times of worship, we ought to be found prostrating before God in His presence. Worship is the key to hearing the voice of God because worship ushers us into His presence where he speaks.

To hear the voice of God through the Holy Spirit, you must learn to practice the presence of God that means to live in His presence daily. Worship is the highest level of prayer. Worship is the highest level of ecstasy. Worship is the highest level of intimacy. You will never fully understand the heart of God on a personal level until you practice deep, intimate worship.

As you begin to grow in worship, you will begin to grow in God. Worship will bring you into oneness with God the Father, God the Son, and God the Holy Spirit. I've never seen someone come out of true worship and remain the same. In worship, God's nature becomes your nature, meaning that you develop His character, attributes, personality, and His nature.

Worship will release an anointing that's transformative which makes it impossible to remain in a carnal state of mind. Worship will prepare you for a God visitation, a Jesus visitation, a glory visitation, an angelic visitation. A visitation is the appearance or coming of a supernatural influence or spirit. You can be visited by Jesus or by an angel or even demons.

Worship will prepare your spirit to become sensitive to the eternal realm, either good or bad. One of the greatest ways to exercise your spiritual senses, is to practice worship daily. Worship gives us access to the throne room as in Psalm 103:19, "The Lord hath prepared his throne in the heavens; and his kingdom ruleth over all." It is out of the throne room where the Father begins to allow the River of Life to flow from His throne to Earth.

Revelations 22:1-2 states, "And he shewed me a pure river of water of life, clear as crystal, proceeding out of the throne of God and of the Lamb. In the midst of the street of it, and on either side of the river, was there the tree of life, which bare twelve manner of fruits, and yielded her fruit every month: and the leaves of the tree were for the healing of the nations..." (also see Ezekiel 47:1-12). In this river there is healing, miracles, deliverance, breakthrough, love, joy, peace, and much more. As you begin to worship, this powerful river will begin to flow right where you are and supernaturally, life is brought to every dead thing in your life.

Worship will open heaven's portal over your life, over your finances, over your ministry, and over your purpose and destiny. The purpose of worship is to bring heaven to you.

Worship will unlock the prophetic realm, the angelic realm, the healing realm, the miracle realm, the glory realm and revelation realms. Revelation realms include the dream realm, the vision realm, and the prophetic realm. As you continue to read this chapter, my heart's desire is that God the Father will begin to release the spirit of worship upon you.

You must understand that worship is not an event, worship is a lifestyle. Worship and character are inseparable. It's impossible to effectively engage in pure worship without character according to John 4:24, "God is a Spirit: and they that worship him must worship him in spirit and in truth." That word *truth* in Greek, *Aletheia,* means character.

It is pure character that produces true worship. God sees your worship as valuable to Him when it is a worship from a person of character. I find that there is a people that do not have character; yet, they seek to worship God. The Bible says in Proverbs 15:8, "The sacrifice of the wicked is an abomination to the Lord: but the prayer of the upright is his delight." Therefore, God cannot accept any sacrifice, praise, or worship from someone that is wicked. An abomination is anything that offends God.

The Bible talks about how the priests were offering bread that was polluted on the altar according to Malachi 1:7, "Ye offer polluted bread upon mine altar; and ye say, Wherein have we polluted thee? In that ye say, The table of the Lord is contemptible." They were giving a sacrifice that was not pleasing to God, and God refused to accept what they were offering God something from a polluted place. Whenever we give God the offering of praise and worship, it becomes abominable when the sacrifice is coming from a wicked heart.

Matthew 5:8 says, "Blessed are the pure in heart: for they shall see God." *Pure,* or the Greek *Katharos,* means consecrated, purified, free from corruption desires. For

your worship to be acceptable to God, there
must be a purification that takes place. No
purification, no pure worship.

The first step to presenting a pure worship
before the Lord is to purify ourselves
mentally, physically, and spiritually (see
Genesis 4:3-5). It wasn't the offering God had
a problem with in this verse. God took issue
with Cain's Spiritual heart condition. We
know this because God told Cain, "if thou
doest well would not thou be accepted?"

The reason why God did not accept Cain's
offering was because Cain never dealt with
his internal issues. When he went to present
his offering to the Lord, God rejected his
sacrifice (See Proverbs 15:8). When
character is in alignment with God, then will
God receive that which you're offering to
Him.

Worship, or the Greek *Proskynéō,* means to
bow down, to prostrate oneself, to adore, and
to revere. When Jesus was in the wilderness

according to Matthew 4: 8-9, "Satan the tempter came to tempt him and said, "If thou wilt fall down and worship me, I will give you all the kingdoms of the world and the glory of them."

Satan was after one thing, and that was the worship. Even from the beginning, Satan was trying to steal the worship and even today Satan is steal attempting to steal the worship. Because if he can steal your worship, he can rob you of your relationship with God. His assignment is to keep you from worship because God lives in the worship.

God responds to the worshipper. God is attracted to the worshipper. The Bible says in John 4:24, "But the hour is coming, and now is, when the true worshipers will worship the Father in spirit and truth; for the Father is seeking such to worship Him. God is Spirit, and those who worship Him must worship in spirit and truth." It is one thing to seek after God, but it is a whole other thing when God is seeking after you. The way to get God's attention to seek after you is to become a worshipper in His kingdom.

God is calling us to worship. The Bible said in the book of Revelation, chapter 2, verse 13, " I know thy works, and where thou dwellest, even where Satan's seat is: and thou holdest fast my name, and hast not denied my faith, even in those days wherein Antipas was my faithful martyr, who was slain among you, where Satan dwelleth." The text shows us that even Satan was in God's house - the church. Satan is not going to come where access hasn't been given to him. When you build yourself an idol, it gives Satan permission and access to invade that particular space so he can come and receive his worship.

John 5:21 offers, "Little children, keep yourselves from idols." There is a word in Greek, *idololatriah*. It's where the English word idolatry originates. Idolatry means image worship, idol worship, and the worship of false gods. Idolatry is anything that you place before God.

Now if Satan had a seat in the synagogue this indicates that the leaders in this church allowed him to become comfortable there. And so how is it that he's sitting among the believers? It's only through idol worship that gave Satan access to take a seat and to abide among them. You must understand that he does not belong in the house of God, the temple belongs to God. Through idolatry we give Satan a seat of authority in the church.

The word worship comes from an old English word worth-ship. Worth-ship simply means to acknowledge the worth or the value of something. When we worship God, we are acknowledging His worth, His values, His power, His dominion and His glory.

When you show me a worshipper, you show me an effective believer, a man or woman of power, a man or woman that is living a life disciplined to worship. Worship will create an environment for God visitation. Worship will create an environment for glory visitation and for angelic visitation. That's why worship is so powerful.

We read in Genesis 2:15, "And the Lord God took the man, and put him into the Garden of Eden to dress it and to keep it." The word *dress*, or the Hebrew word *abad,* means to worship and to cultivate. Adam was cultivating a place for God to visit, dwell and to abide. When was the last time you began to cultivate an environment for a visitation of God? When was the last time you cultivated a place for angelic visitation or visitation of Jesus?

A place prepared for visitation is a place that's been cultivated and prepared for a supernatural invasion. But what we have done is we have allowed ourselves to be distracted by the noise and by the cares of this world not knowing that Jesus said in 1 John 2:15, "Love not the world, neither the things that are in the world." David said according to 2 Corinthians 6:17, "Wherefore come out from among them, and be ye separate, saith the Lord, and touch not the unclean thing; and I will receive you."

God says in 1 Peter 1:16," Because it is written, Be ye holy; for I am holy." Holiness simply means to be separated from sin and therefore consecrated unto God. Holiness speaks of God divine nature and character. That means that we are striving every day to become more like God because God only responds to Himself. So why should God respond to the language in which your speaking if you do not sound like Him?

He watches over His word. God responds to His word. That's the problem with the church today the church is ministering a different sound or language, that sound is a familiar and strange sound that does not sound like God. That's why when the Hebrew boys were subdued to go into the Babylonian captivity, the king wanted everything in the kingdom at the sound of the music to bow down and worship the image.

But if you notice the reason why the Hebrew boys found themselves in trouble with the king was because when everybody began to bow down to the sound, they refused (see Daniel 3:10-19). My issue with the body of Christ is that many are bowing down to a Babylonian, perverted, demonic sound that does not sound like God. That's why I can understand when Paul said in 1 Corinthians 14:8, "For if the trumpet gives an uncertain sound, who shall prepare himself to the battle?"

They're acting just like the sons of Aaron when they were in the temple rendering before the Lord strange fire (see Leviticus 10:1). "And Nadab and Abihu, the sons of Aaron, took either of them his censer, and put fire therein, and put incense thereon, and offered strange fire before the Lord, which he commanded them not." The word strange in the Hebrew *zuwr*, means foreign profane, and unauthorized. They were taking stuff from the world and they were mixing it the temple. Anytime you take worldly or secular things and mix it with God produces strange fire. God is too holy to be mixed.

We have musicians coming to church and they're taking worldly chords and playing them in the church. Nobody has any discernment to identify that which is authentic and real. But I believe that God is getting ready to raise up and restore the true Kingdom sound. I believe that God is getting ready to raise up a pure worship like we've never seen before.

Why is worship important? Worship is important because worship will create an environment that is conducive for healing, glory encounters, signs, wonders, and miracles. For some of you that have ask the question why is it that we don't see the miraculous signs of God in our churches of today? It's only because we have allowed the enemy to cause our worship to become distorted.

You cannot expect God to divinely intervene into your life if your worship is contaminated. There must be a worship that's pure before the Lord. When Gideon got ready to go into battle, he started off with 22,000 men and the Lord said to Gideon, "You have too many men." So, 22,000 was decreased to 10,000. The Lord said, "Gideon you still have too many men..." (Judges 7:3-8).

The Lord gave Gideon instructions to have the men drink from a river. All the men that were lapping like dogs were the men that God chose to use in battle. Remember the word worship *Proskunéō* means to lie flat, to bow down, and to prostrate oneself. But that word *Proskunéō* also means to lick like a dog licking his master's hand.

The 300 men that were with Gideon, were lapping like dogs, metaphorically, were the worshipers that God had chosen to go into battle. You must understand that in order for you to prevail in battle, opposition, and adversity in which you're going through, you must learn how to worship from a pure heart. Worship is a powerful strategy that causes God to divinely intervene in your situation and fix your problem. Worship provokes God to become the prevailing factor in your life, despite what you're going through.

In the Garden of Eden, God would come and visit Adam every day. The Bible said in Genesis 3:9, "And the Lord God called unto Adam, and said unto him, Where art thou?" As long as Adam was a worshipper, Adam was exposed to the voice of God every day. Only a worshipper is exposed to the voice of God. Because God speaks in worship.

Why does He speak in worship? Because worship ushers us into a realm of His presence where He speaks. Worship prepares your spirit to receive revelatory deposits. Being a praiser is not enough. Praise creates God a house, but worship brings God into that house.

Worship provokes God to speak, to heal, and to restore. Worship stimulates the supernatural power of God to manifest in your life. As a worshipper, Adam was exposed to the presence of God. How do I know? Genesis 3:8 tells us, "And they heard the voice of the Lord God walking in the garden in the cool of the day: and Adam and his wife hid themselves from the presence of the Lord God amongst the trees of the garden."

So technically, before the fall of Adam, Adam was having a face to face relationship with God as he was hearing the voice of the Lord. Show me someone that God dwells in, then you show me someone that is a true worshipper. You must understand that the glory has always been attracted to worshippers.

Glory is married to the worshipper, His bride. God is looking for true worshippers in these last days whose hearts are in love with

Him. The moment you become
a worshipper you will then live your
life carrying the glory mantle. You've got to
become the worshipper for God to respond
to you. When you become
a worshipper, God seeks to find you as His
bride.

The Bible says that God visits man every
morning (see Job 7:18). That word *morning*,
or the Hebrew word *boqer*, means morning
watch which is between the hours of 2 am
and sunrise. That is God's time to visit
mankind whether male or female. God can
come whenever he wants, but this verse
confirms that this is God's time to visit man.

I believe according to the scripture that God's
special time to visit mankind in the earth is in
the early morning hours. That's why it's
imperative that we seek the Lord in worship
throughout the early hours of the day,
because it is God's time of visitation. You
want to hear what God is saying, then seek
him in early morning hours.

This is the reason why Christ ministry was so
successful according to Mark 1:35, "And in
the morning, rising up a great while before
day, he went out, and departed into a solitary
place, and there prayed." Jesus believed in
getting up early.

Fervent prayer and intercession ought to be
engaged during this time because a lot
of spiritual activity goes on in the
early morning hours. Witches and warlocks g
et up around about this time practicing their
demonic rituals.

Job 10:12 says, "Thou hast granted me life
and favour, and thy visitation hath preserved
my spirit." God desire for us all to be
visited by Him because it's in these visitations
where you are preserved. That word preserve
comes from the Hebrew word *shamar* which
means to guard, protect, and watch over.

It's amazing how we say we've been in God's
presence, but we never hear Him speak. It

amazes me how we say we've been in worship, but we don't know what God is saying. Moses was with God for 40 days. The bible shows us that when Moses came down from the mountain the people had saw that the glory of God was shining upon his face Exodus 34:35, "And the children of Israel saw the face of Moses, that the skin of Moses' face shone: and Moses put the vail upon his face again, until he went in to speak with him..." (see also 2 Corinthians 3:13).

The glory of God that radiated from his face was an indication that the prophet had been with God. I'm so tired of people saying that they've been with God but they're coming out with no substance, no power, and no revelation. When the children of Israel came out of Egypt the Bible said, "They came out with great substance (see Gen 15:14). It's imperative that when you come out of His presence that you come out with power, with answers, with victory, with a word from the Lord for the nations.

God is looking for somebody that He can speak to and that person is the worshipper. God reveals His secrets and mysteries to the worshipper. This is the reason why the enemy has been attacking your mind, your flesh, your marriage, your business, because one thing the enemy hates is a true worshipper.

The purpose of worship is to create an environment for angelic visitation. The more you worship the more God begins to release angels to assist you in the earth. We must understand that angels were created to serve us.

According to Hebrews 1:14, "Are they not all ministering spirits, sent forth to minister for them who shall be heirs of salvation?" Angels were created to assist you. And so, the more you worship God, the more God then begins to release assigned angels to assist and serve you in the earthly realm.

The word angel comes from a Hebrew word

malak which means a messenger and ambassador. What is an ambassador? An ambassador is one who is the head of an embassy. An embassy is made up of a group of officials that represent their government in a foreign country. So, angels as ambassadors represent the embassy of the kingdom of God on earth.

As I've mentioned earlier, worship unlocks the angelic realm. Where there is worship, there will always be angelic activity. Worshippers know that they are not fighting battles alone. And so, you don't have to live your life being perplexed and confused by that which the enemy is trying to disrupt in your life. You must understand that there is nothing that the enemy can possibly do to a worshipper, a true worshipper. That's why worship is so powerful and effective because it's something that the enemy cannot do.

The reason why Satan fights you so strongly is because when he sees you worship God, he sees that you're doing what he once did when he lived in Heaven. His ministry was in the area of music. Why do you think the enemy attacks the music department in the churches? Because if he can distort the worship leader from producing a kingdom sound in the church, he can then hinder the Spirit of God from moving.

Lucifer had a great ability to produce powerful music in Heaven. So, his strategy and plan was to pervert music by perverting the worshipper. God saw that Lucifer had messed up in heaven as a worshipper and God gave this responsibility to man to worship God on earth.

Satan sees that there has been an exchange. God has taking his responsibility had has given it to a man. I believe out of jealousy Satan went into the Garden of Eden with the intentions to distort Adam's relationship with God which was his worship. Now man is out of relationship with God.

So now, Jesus makes it His purpose to come

to earth to redeem and to restore what Adam lost. Now that Jesus has restored what Adam lost, the Devil once again is walking about seeking whom he may devour as we see in 1 Peter 5:8, "Be sober, be vigilant; because your adversary the devil, as a roaring lion, walketh about, seeking whom he may devour." He's still looking for a worship that he can pervert.

But it is your responsibility to guard your worship, to guard your praise. This is the thing that belongs to you that the enemy seeks so diligently to contaminate. And the way he contaminates it is by contaminating your life. Whatever you do, you must understand that you cannot afford to allow the enemy to steal your worship.

There was a woman in the bible that had ten coins. One of the coins she lost in the house. We read in Luke 15:8-9, "Either what woman having ten pieces of silver, if she lose one piece, doth not light a candle, and sweep the house, and seek diligently till she find it?

9 And when she hath found it, she calleth her friends and her neighbours together, saying, Rejoice with me; for I have found the piece which I had lost."

This coin is still missing in some churches and that coin is worship. That woman did not find that coin until she *swept her house clean.* There's some things that you got to clean out of the attic of your mind and out of the basement of your spirit for you to find that pure worship that's locked inside of you. It is the enemy's assignment to cause you to lose that coin. But whatever you do, do not compromise your worship.

A king has access to the kingdom, but a priest has access to the throne room. What gives them access to the throne room is the key of worship. That is why Paul the apostle of Jesus Christ said according to Philippians 3:10, "That I may know him, and the power of his resurrection, and the fellowship of his sufferings, being made conformable unto his death." And the word *fellowship,* or the

Greek *koinónia,* means intimacy. God uses trials in a way to perfect the worship or relationship with God through pain and hardship.

Like Eli's sons, they were priest, yet they did not know the Lord. According to 1 Samuel 2:12, "Now the sons of Eli were sons of Belial; they knew not the Lord." It is possible to be religious and yet, not know the Lord. How is it that your singing songs of the Lord but you don't know Him? How is it that your speaking in tongues and shouting, but you do not know Him? The answer is, many have religion, but they have no relationship with God.

Only those that know Him intimately can be validated as true worshippers of God. Worship is what gives us access to the throne room where God abides. In Revelation 4:10, we read, "the four and twenty elders fall down before Him that sits on the throne, and worship Him that liveth for ever and ever, and cast their crowns before the throne." The

24 elders bow down before the Lord and they began to sing songs of worship before the Lord and they cast down their crowns which represents their glory.

There are some steps before God allows you to enter into the realm of pure worship. That is to say, there are some things that you need to leave behind. There are some things that you need to remove from you. There are some things you need to get delivered from. There are some things you need to disconnect yourself from for God to share himself fully with you, meaning His thoughts, His heart, and His presence in worship.

First thing the 24 elders did was cast down their crowns. There's some stuff in your life that you must cast down. There's some stuff in your life that you must amputate to go to the next level of worship. You cannot afford to have things in your life that you value more than God. Our flesh can be wicked, tricking us to idolize things more than God. God doesn't want anything put before Him.

We see this in Exodus 20:3, "Thou shalt have no other gods before me."

One of the reasons why God tested Abraham with Isaac was so that he could make sure that Abraham did not love Isaac (blessing) more than God (the blesser). Every now and then, God has to test you with your Isaac. You must ensure you don't love your Isaac more than you love God. Because if God sees that you're loving Isaac more than Him, I promise you God will take Isaac from you.

And so, it's important that you make sure that you put God over Isaac and not Isaac over God.

It amazes me how we spend more time with Isaac than God. It amazes me how we're more intimate with Isaac than God. It amazes me how we can love and cherish Isaac more than we love and cherish God. But I believe that there's a people that God is raising up that's willing to lose Isaac to have more God.

He wants to make sure that you're not

worshipping Isaac more than worshipping Him. So, God has to test you. Questions we ask: Why did God take the house from me? Why did God cause me to lose the car? Because God saw that you were putting Isaac before Him. Abraham waited 25 years for this promise. What did you do when God tests you with the very thing that He promised you? Whatever you do, do not allow yourself to put Isaac before God.

Worship will create an atmosphere that is conducive for healing. The Greek word for worship *therapeuo* is where we get the English word therapeutic. Therapeutic is a medical term which means to heal or cure. Do you not know that worship is like a medicine? Worship will cause sick bodes to be supernaturally healed when worship is being practiced. Worship will release healing angels to heal sickness and diseases.

There is power in worship. Remember, worship gives us access to the healing realm. That's why when you when you go to Benny

Hinn services, you see masses of people being supernaturally healed. Why? Because he understood how to create an atmosphere of healing through worship.

Worship will literally release the angels of healing to come to you. You don't have to wait for the pastor to lay hands on you for healing. You don't have to wait for the prophet to come and lay hands on you for healing. Right where you are, begin to worship Him and worship itself will begin to release the angels of healing or Jesus to heal you.

Worship gives angels assignments to heal the sick. I don't care what you need - it could be financial breakthrough, worship will cause angels of prosperity to come into your life. That is the power of worship. Listen, beloved - whatever you do, do not lose your worship. As a priestly people you're mandated to live a lifestyle of worship. I said it earlier, Worship is who I am. Worship is who you are.

God is getting ready to do something in the earth that is so powerful, and it's going to be ushered through hungry, spirit-filled worshippers. When Jesus fed the 5000, not including the women and the children, Jesus told the disciples to gather the fragments. According to John 6:12, "When they were filled, he said unto his disciples, Gather up the fragments that remain, that nothing be lost."

That word *fragment,* or the Greek *klasma,* means broken pieces. God told the disciples to gather the broken pieces. Why gather the broken pieces? Because God specializes in broken pieces. The people that are broken, God is getting ready to gather, and make them whole and raise them up as worshippers. And these worshippers are going to cause the glory of God to begin to invade the earth.

And it's at that moment which we will see one of the greatest revivals like we have never seen before, but you must be found as a worshipper. There is nothing more important than your relationship with God.

You must to remember what Jesus said - "You prophesied in my name, cast out demons in my name and did miracles in my name but I never knew you." Matthews 7:22 continues to illustrate this point, "Many will say to me in that day, Lord, Lord, have we not prophesied in thy name? And in thy name have cast out devils? And in thy name done many wonderful works?"

Why did He say, "I never knew you"? That word *knew* refers to intimacy or relationship. These were people that were doing ministry but they had no relationship with God because they were not worshippers. When God said I never knew you, that confirmed that they weren't worshippers. The bible said Adam knew Eve, (see Genesis 4:1), which means that he knew her intimately. Worship is spiritual intercourse, or connection, with God. We want a microwave, quick, and easy type of relationship.

God has opened the door of His bedchamber and is waiting on His bride to come in and spend time with Him. According to the Jewish custom, the way they would establish the marriage was by way of consummation. Isn't it amazing how God has a bride that doesn't want to consummate with him because we're so occupied doing other things in life?

We're chasing after other gods and God is saying as your husband, "I'm longing for my queen. I'm looking for my bride to come and spend intimate time with me". Yet, we spend so much time doing other things that are insignificant and idle and God is saying, "Where is she? Where is my wife?"

And then sometimes we have the audacity to get mad at God when God begins to disrupt our lives, causing us to go through all types of trouble and painful experiences just to gain our attention. God loves you so much that

He will allow you to go through some tough things in life just to bring you back to Him. Remember God said, "Adam where art you?" (See Genesis 3:9.)

It wasn't that God didn't know where Adam was because God is omniscient which means He's all knowing. Just wasn't in his intimate place with God. God is saying the same thing today - where is my church, where is my people, where is my bride? God is beseeching many TO COME BACK TO WORSHIP.

CHAPTER 4

The Cloud of Glory

If you're hungry for the next dimension in God, I suggest to you to prepare yourself for a glory revelation. This chapter will give you a greater understanding of the glory cloud. There are many scriptures in the Bible that speak about the glory cloud, both in the Old and New Testament. The glory cloud is a subject that many religious minds refuse to talk about due to their disbelief that it is possible for a supernatural cloud to appear among us.

The cloud appeared in the wilderness among the Israelites (see Exodus 33:9). God is no respecter of person. As Israel saw the mighty acts of God, God also desires for us to experience His manifested acts, signs and wonders in our lifetime (see Psalm 103:7). This chapter is going to challenge your theology. I know that in the last days, God is going to prove this chapter to be true concerning the descension of the glory cloud.

The word *cloud,* or the Hebrew word *anan,* means fog or smoke. This theophanic cloud can come in the form of a fog or smoke. In times of intense worship, God desires to manifest Himself in the cloud, which will come in the form or fog or smoke.

Question: Has this happened before? Absolutely! There are churches that were so hungry for God, and their worship was so intense, that the glory cloud manifested before their eyes in the form of a fog or smoke.

God's great pleasure is to manifest the glory cloud to you too but there must be a hunger and desperation in you for more of God. Before I continue this chapter, I would like to interject and share a brief testimony concerning the glory cloud I experienced. I cannot remember the date that it happened, I only remember the experience.

One particular day, the presence of God was so strong upon me. I felt an unusual presence from God that was stronger than normal. When I went to bed that night, I couldn't stop physically shaking under the power of God's presence. I knew that God was doing something supernatural. It was truly a day of visitation for me.

When I fell asleep, suddenly, it was like I was in midair. Like Paul the Apostle, I didn't know if I was in my physical body or out my body in this eternal place (see 2 Corinthians 12:2). I remember standing in midair with no floor beneath me, weeping in the presence of God. God was above me, but I was not allowed to look upon Him. I then began to look around as I was weeping, and I noticed that I was inside of a cloud with the Lord. When I woke up, I knew that my spirit had been caught up. I knew that I had been in an eternal realm.

God Lives in the Cloud

In my experience, I noticed that God was with me in the cloud. I learned a few years later, that according to the scriptures, God dwells in the cloud. We can read this in 1 Kings 8:12, Psalm 18:11, Exodus 19:9, and Psalm 99:7. When I discovered this in the Bible, these scriptures brought clarity to my divine encounter. Now, everything finally made sense to me concerning the reason why I was standing before God in the midst of a cloud.

Now that you have this revelation, without fear begin to ask God to grant you this privilege to join Him in the glory cloud. The

Prophet Moses had this privilege of entering into the cloud with God in Exodus 24:18.

The religious mind would say this isn't possible. However, there are three facts to consider. 1. This proof is in the Bible. 2. Prophet Moses was a human that had this supernatural experience. 3. Prophet Moses did not die in the cloud. The apostles Peter, James, and John also entered into the cloud of glory according to Luke 9:34.
They were mortal men, like Moses, that had this glory cloud experience, and they too did not die.

My hunger is not only to see the glory cloud, but like these mighty men of God, I want to enter the glory cloud. I believe that God has given me this revelation to write it in this book, so that the Body of Christ may experience this wonderful encounter with God in the cloud. Revelations are the keys to unlock realms.

Now use this key of knowledge and unlock

the realm that gives you access to enter the cloud of glory. My prayer is that God grants you this experience. I believe that like me, as you enter this cloud, your life will never be the same again. In the cloud you will experience impartation, revelation, transformation, and manifestations. So, if Moses, Peter, James and John entered the cloud so can you.

God Descending in the Cloud

Many times, in the scriptures, God would come down in a cloud and talk with Prophet Moses. In Exodus 34:5, we read, "And the Lord descended in the cloud, and stood with him there, and proclaimed the name of the Lord..." (Also read Exodus 33:9, Numbers 11:17, Numbers 11:25, and Numbers 12:5).

God the Father wants to come down again in a cloud to make known His manifested presence amongst His people. I know this may seem impossible, and your mind will never process this truth with a logical mindset. Logic will never agree with revelation.

Many of us have been convinced to believe that if we encounter God on earth, in a cloud, that we would die. Don't allow this erroneous belief to hinder you from experiencing God on another level. Question: Did Prophet Moses and the Apostles Peter, James and John die when God appeared unto them in a cloud? Absolutely not. My point is that you can have this experience too.

Prophet Moses not only saw the cloud that surrounds God but he also saw the form or image of God. According to Numbers 12:8, "With him will I speak mouth to mouth, even apparently, and not in dark speeches; and the similitude of the Lord shall he behold: wherefore then were ye not afraid to speak against my servant Moses?" In the King James Version, the word *similitude* is used, which in the Hebrew *temunah* means form. When Prophet Moses entered the cloud of glory, he was honored to see the form of God.

One day, God decided to walk in the Garden of Eden in the cool of the day according to Genesis 3:8. So if God was walking in the garden, that means God came down to earth. God also came down to see the Tower of Babel and the city the people were building in Genesis 11:5. God came down in the wilderness, in the Garden of Eden, and as the people were building the Tower of Babel. Now God wants to come down again in our generation in the glory cloud and dwell amongst His people. I hope I'm sparking a greater hunger in you to experience God in a much deeper way.

God Speaks from the Cloud

When God came down in a cloud, he spoke from the cloud. Whenever God got ready to speak to Prophet Moses, He would come down and speak from the cloud (see Exodus 19:9, also read Psalm 99:7, Numbers 12:5 and Exodus 24:16). When Jesus took the Apostles Peter, James and John on Mount

Transfiguration, God came down and spoke to Peter from the cloud (Luke 9:35).

God always speaks from His presence. As we live in the realm of God's presence, we learn the sound of His voice when He speaks. We should be practicing the presence of God daily. This is how we hear instructions from the Holy Spirit who channels the voice of God.

As we follow those instructions given to us by the Holy Spirit, it keeps us in the will of God because we are doing what the Father desires for us to do. You will never see the plan of God with clarity concerning your life if you neglect time spent in God's presence. You should not make a sudden move or decision without first receiving divine instructions from the Lord.

Moving without divine instructions will eventually lead to failure, defeat, and discouragement. The pain that we feel when our visions, dreams, plans and ideas fail pulls us into a cave of depression. Then, we find ourselves playing the blame game. Who do we blame? Most of the time we blame God not realizing that we've failed ourselves for not first consulting God.

In the wilderness, the Israelites followed the cloud, which represented God's manifested presence. Living in the Father's presence keeps us from being misled or misguided by the flesh. It takes faith to obey the still, small voice of the Holy Spirit. Without faith, we will rely upon our own senses and instinct.

Most of the time God's instructions and goals for us seem impossible, unattainable, and unachievable. The flesh tells us to do what makes sense to us and this is how we miss the move of God in our lives. Spending time in God's presence helps us to grow sensitive to the character of His spirit and the voice of the Spirit. Oftentimes, we may hear the voice of the Spirit, but refuse to obey.

Like Jonah, he heard the voice of God telling

him to go to Nineveh, but he refused to obey.
Like Prophet Jonah, many of us were
swallowed up by the fish of disappointment
due to disobedience. If you hear the voice of
God giving you instructions, OBEY (see
Isaiah 1:19).

I've learned that God loves to visit his
servants on mountains. With Prophet Moses
it was Mount Sinai in Exodus 19:9, "And the
Lord said unto Moses, Lo, I come unto thee
in a thick cloud, that the people may hear
when I speak with thee, and believe thee
forever. And Moses told the words of the
people unto the Lord." With Jesus, it was on
Mount Transfiguration (see Luke 9:34-35).

You don't need a physical mountain. Your
living room, bedroom, closet or even praying
on the altar at your local church can be your
mountain. Whatever is comfortable for you
to spend time with God, without distractions,
can be your mountain.

Your mountain is your spiritual place of

appointment between you and God. God is waiting on you to get to your mountain so that He can speak with you. The still, small voice of the spirit of God came to Elijah on Mount Horeb (see 1 Kings 19:11-13). The Bible also explains how the voice of God was walking in the Garden of Eden. According to Genesis 3:8, "And they heard the voice of the Lord God walking in the garden in the cool of the day: and Adam and his wife hid themselves from the presence of the Lord God amongst the trees of the garden." So, if the voice of God was walking in the Garden of Eden, this indicates that God's power, presence, and glory was there also. Remember, God speaks from His glory and presence.

Glory Portal

A portal is a gateway, doorway, entryway that gives access for the supernatural to engage or manifest on earth. When a spiritual portal is open, theophanic angels have access to you without any demonic interference. Not all portals are good portals, there are also demonic portals.

Demonic portals are created when satanic agents, such as witches and warlocks find a place to practice their demonic rituals. Sometimes, they find their place in mountains to worship Satan. As satanic agents begin to practice their rituals, demonic portals open giving demonic activities and influences access to bring trouble and warfare to your life.

This is the reason why God desires for His children to pray and fast often to effectively war against the powers of darkness. Prayer and fasting opens heavens' portals over your life. When a portal is open, God sends angels, visions, dreams, miracles, and supernatural breakthroughs to you.

One day, Jacob fell asleep on a stone and had a powerful spiritual dream. He saw a ladder that reached the heavens and he saw the Lord standing above it and angels (see Genesis 28:11-22). When Jacob had awakened, he called the city Luz "the Gate of Heaven". Jacob realized that there was a portal open over the city of Luz. When he came into this revelation, he called the city Bethel meaning the house of God. Where there is a portal, there is a lot of angelic activity and supernatural manifestations.

There's a particular mountain I want to pull your focus to and that is Mount Sinai or Mount Horeb. I discovered many years ago that these mountains were one and the same. God had summoned the Prophet Moses to come up to Mount Sinai so that he could speak to him.

When Elijah was fleeing from the wicked Jezebel, his journey was to go to Mount Horeb, the same place God spoke to Prophet Moses. The reason why Elijah the Prophet went to Mount Horeb was because he knew that a portal was still open over the mountain. When he got to Mount Horeb, God was still there. I call this a glory portal. The reason why I call this mountain a glory portal is because where God is, there will also be glory.

As you meet with God daily in the same place, eventually, a glory portal is going to open. Depending on the intensity of your time spent in prayer and your sacrifice of fasting before the Lord. I desire to see glory portals open over America but how is that going to happen? When the body of Christ, the ecclesia, the church, the Assembly of God unite in prayer and fasting. Then will we see the spirit of revival fall on our nation.

People of God let us unite in prayer and fasting so that we all can experience a great outpour of God's spirit. Let's get hungry for God and unlock glory portals over our cities and nations. It's time for our nations to experience angelic manifestations, Jesus visitations, miracles, signs and wonders, supernatural healing, and deliverance. Let us come together and destroy the powers of darkness. It's time for the world to experience a mighty outpour of the glory and spirit of God on earth.

Glory Fire

The glory cloud is more than just a fog or
smoke, the glory cloud can also come in the
form of fire according to Exodus 13:21,
"Then Moses called for all the elders of
Israel, and said unto them, Draw out and
take you a lamb according to your families,
and kill the Passover." If you notice that by
night, the cloud lead the Israelites by a pillar
of fire. **THAT'S GLORY FIRE!**

Let's also look at Deuteronomy 4: 11-12,
"And ye came near and stood under the
mountain; and the mountain burned with fire
unto the midst of heaven, with darkness,
clouds, and thick darkness. 12 And the Lord
spake unto you out of the midst of the fire: ye
heard the voice of the words, but saw no
similitude; only ye heard a voice."

The Bible explains that the mountain was
burning with fire and was surrounded by a
thick cloud. Verse 12 reveals that God spoke

to Prophet Moses from the midst of the fire.
THAT'S GLORY FIRE.

Let us also journey to Exodus 3:2-4, "And
the angel of the Lord appeared unto him in a
flame of fire out of the midst of a bush: and
he looked, and, behold, the bush burned
with fire, and the bush was not consumed. 3
And Moses said, I will now turn aside, and
see this great sight, why the bush is not burnt.
4 And when the Lord saw that he turned
aside to see, God called unto him out of the
midst of the bush, and said, Moses, Moses.
And he said, Here am I." I find it amazing,
supernatural, and theophanic that the bush
was on fire but it did not consume. **THAT'S
GLORY FIRE.**

When the glory cloud shows up like the
burning bush, the glory will not consume
you. But it will consume everything that is not
righteous or holy. The glory fire is a purifier.
The glory will burn lust, pride, hatred,
unforgiveness, resentment, curses, witchcraft,
hexes and spells.

The kingdom of darkness is ineffective to operate when the glory fire is present. We must pray for glory fire to fall. God desires to surround your homes, churches, children, marriages, and you as an individual with glory fire. As Kingdom citizens, we are supposed to be carrying glory fire as in Hebrews 1:7, "And of the angels he saith, Who maketh his angels spirits, and his ministers a flame of fire."

When we preach, teach, prophesy, sing or witness to someone about the testimony of Jesus Christ, glory fire should fall on the person to whom we are ministering. That soul should be consumed and saturated with so much glory that we shall see instant transformation without process. That's supernatural!

When we come together to pray, the atmosphere should be charged and infused with glory fire. What we read in the Bible should become our everyday reality. God is the same God yesterday, today and forever more. No one should leave your presence the same when you are a carrier of glory fire.

God is a consuming fire according to Hebrews 12:29. So if God is a consuming fire, and your life is filled with the fullness of God, according to Ephesians 3:19 the moment you open your mouth and speak of Jesus Christ, glory fire should fall and fill the place you've entered. This only happens when your life is sold out to God and your mind, body, and soul are discipled to prayer, fasting, consecration, and obedience to the call of God on your life.

The manifested presence of God will always follow the humble, the broken, and the obedient. It is time for the Father's presence to become your presence. The purpose of fire is to consume and burn up. I always tell people that there cannot be a fire unless there is a sacrifice. If you give God a worthy sacrifice, God will give you in return glory fire (See 1 Kings 18:38).

Prayer is a great sacrifice. Revival has always been birthed on the wings of prayer. But what is prayer without commitment? Jesus Christ was committed to prayer and as a result he demonstrated the power of God effectively.

I must be honest, you must learn how to stretch yourselves in prayer. What does this mean? Praying longer than the length of time you normally pray. Sometimes, we have to pray until we get a prayer through. *Praying Through Determines Breakthrough.*
Fasting is also a great sacrifice. Many avoid this subject due to the hunger pains fasting brings, but fasting causes our prayers to be answered expeditiously. I understand that it's not easy to fast, but it is a powerful key to unlocking the realm of glory. This is a key to glory fire.

If Jesus came to earth as our propitiation, the atoning sacrifice for us, then I believe we should find time and disciple to sacrifice a few days in fasting before the Lord. We must die to our flesh so that the power of God can destroy the yokes of bondage, curses and sins. Both prayer and fasting involves a sacrifice of one's own carnal desires.

The primary purpose of dying to self is to crucify the carnal man, Adamic nature. Dying to self is a metaphor for bringing your body under the control and power of the Holy Spirit. This helps us to take on the characteristics of Christ, His righteousness and holiness. Prayer and fasting will prepare you for a glory fire experience.

Prophet Moses experienced glory fire and now it's time for you to experience glory fire. God wants to release glory fire all over the nation. Can you imagine seeing cities, states, and nations consumed and mantled in glory fire? In Acts 2:3, tongues of fire sat on each of them. The Bible said that the fire appeared. The word appeared, the Greek *Optanomai,* which means to gaze with wide open eyes.

This means they that were in the upper room and saw this fire manifest. Beloved, it's time to see the manifested presence of God in your own personal life. My desire for you is that you live your life seeing into the supernatural. Remember, Jesus saw what his Father was doing according to John 5:19. I pray that our Lord God will release a greater measure of glory fire in our generation. Greater than what Prophet Moses and the children of Israel experienced in the wilderness.

(Glory Fire in Scripture: see Zechariah 2:5, Exodus 24:17, Exodus 13:21, Exodus 3:2).

Glory Defense

The glory of God also serves as a defense. The word defense means the act of protecting, shielding, and guarding against attack, harm and danger. God became a wall of fire around Jerusalem (see Zechariah 2:7). This means that God became Jerusalem's defensive structure. God's glory is also our defensive structure against every attack of the enemy. When our lives become fortified by the glory, no opposing force on the outside will be able to penetrate this glory wall.

I want you to be mindful of what's protecting you in the spirit realm. It's our human nature to believe only what we see. But we serve an invisible God that has established many invisible things such as angels, glory, power, and anointings that protect us.

The Bible says that faith is a shield. We may not see faith as a physical shield but in the spirit, faith is a shield (see Ephesians 6:16). I find confidence and security in my faith in God because I know that my life is protected, shielded, and fortified by the power of God. It's not what you see physically that pleases God, but having faith in Him (see John 20:29).

When you fast, the glory becomes your *reward* which means your rear guard (see Isaiah 58:8). The New Living Translation talks about how the glory of the Lord will protect you from behind. When Prophet Moses brought the Israelites out of Egypt, an army of Egyptians pursued them from behind and as a defense, the pillar of cloud had stood behind the Israelites as their divine protection (see Exodus 14:19). Isn't this very powerful? Hallelujah! What God did for Prophet Moses, He wants to do for you too. God is the same God yesterday, today, and forever more.

The scripture says for upon all, the glory shall be a defense (see Isaiah 4:5). The glory can be a defense over your family, your business, your ministry, your career, your health, and your marriage. This promise is not only for the Israelites, this promise is for you too if you're joint in covenant with God as a New Testament believer.

The word *defense* in the Hebrew *chuppah* means divine protection. If you can receive this revelation by faith, I believe you will begin to approach every situation with a confident, victorious mindset. Know that God, Jesus, Holy Spirit, angels, the blood of Jesus and glory are your divine protection. Knowing this will give you the faith to conquer every challenge in your life.

The Egyptians that are pursuing you from behind can represent sickness, marital problems, financial distress, mental struggles, and depression. I know that there are many more I didn't mention. My point is you serve a mighty God and father who has you covered in every area of your life and has power to deliver you out of trouble (see Psalm 34:19).

CHAPTER 5

Glory Transformation

The sign of true change is internal transformation not external transformation. Most of the time, we spend more energy on changing our external appearance for many erroneous reasons. One primary reason is that sometimes we feel as if we are not pretty or handsome enough. As a result, we begin to develop insecurity issues. So, we spend more time dressing up.

Society has created a false preference that the world seeks to emulate. When we finally conform to the image that society has displayed, through TV, social media, and magazines, we find ourselves still unhappy. We are left with a void and that void is the loss of identity.

I'm not saying not to change the outward appearance, but the outward should be a reflection of the inward. There is a new heart that God wants to give many of you. This new heart is going to give you a new perspective about you.

It is time to take off false labels that people have put on you and put on the garment of holiness. The Bible describes holiness as beautiful (see Psalms 96:9). When God sees that you're living a lifestyle of holiness, this is how God defines true beauty.

Again, nothing wrong with putting on makeup, dressing up in nice clothes, and getting a haircut. But we must come into the realization that we are not defined by aesthetics. We must look like the culture of the kingdom of God.

Transformation is defined as the process of changing. No process, no change. No change, no transformation. I know many of us have heard the term 'process' over and over again. It's a term that we have grown to hate, reject and despise. But, process is necessary. I know you've heard this too.

Process can be long or short but I want to open your eyes to a mystery that the Holy Spirit wants to reveal to you. The glory is transformative. Sometimes the glory can bring instant change without process because everything in the glory realm is now.

Now, change! Now, transformation! Now, Breakthrough! Now, miracle! When Jesus was on Mount Transfiguration, he transfigured instantly (see Matthew 17:2). The word *transfigure* as the Greek *metamorphoo* means to change into another form.

When you encounter the glory of God everything about you will begin to change. Jesus Christ's glorious change began while he was on his knees praying. The Bible says, "and as He prayed, the fashion of his countenance was altered, and His raiment was white and glistering" (see Luke 9:29).

If you notice, Jesus was first in the posture of prayer before this transformation took place. Change always starts with prayer. The apostles Peter, James, and John saw as Jesus was praying instant change. They saw what Jesus would look like in His prophetic future. The apostles saw what Jesus was going to look like after his death.

Prayer and glory will transform you into what you are destined to become. The word *metamorphoo* comes from *morphoo* which speaks of inward change. Your heart must change before you can change your city, state, or nation.

There is a reason why I keep bringing up the heart. The heart was created to be the seat of love. If love becomes your motivation and focus, your intentions will always remain pure.

Like King Saul, God wants to give you a new heart (see 1 Samuel 10:9). The word *heart*, or the Hebrew word *leb*, means mind. So, to have a new heart means to have a new mind. It's impossible to remain with the same old mindset after having a true glory encounter.

Transformed by the Word
Yes, the glory will change you, but to maintain that change, the mind must be renewed by the word of God daily. We read in Romans 12:2, "And be not conformed to this world: but be ye transformed by the renewing of your mind, that ye may prove what is that good, and acceptable, and perfect, will of God." In the natural, if we don't eat, the body will eventually weaken,

shut down, leading to death. This same concept applies spiritually. The Word of God is our spiritual food that keeps us nurtured and strong in the Lord. If we don't eat the Word of God, we will eventually spiritually die.

The devil's plan is to snatch our focus from the Word of God so that we don't study. The devil keeps us distracted by so many carnal things. God wants to restore your hunger and passion for the word of God. For those who've never had a passion for the Word of God, God wants to give you a hunger to study His Word too.

Many in the body of Christ, after experiencing a divine encounter, eventually lose their zeal for God. For that reason, right after the encounter, they find themselves reading the Bible daily, listening to praise and worship music in their homes, and faithful and committed to their local church. Then, suddenly, they begin to lose their zeal and passion for Jesus. They stop reading the

Bible and praying. The devil has deceitfully pulled them away from the holy lifestyle that keep the believer strong. The Bible says without a vision, the people perish (see Proverbs 29:18).

The word *vision* in the Hebrew *chazown* means revelation and prophecy. The word of God is God's revelation and prophecy to man. Without it, we will spiritually perish. We need the revelation of His word daily to change and maintain change. It is revelation that brings about transformation. The word of God is a reflection and revelation of who God is. Jesus was that word, the divine expression of God.

When we study the word of God, that word takes root in your inner soul, spirit, and heart. Your nature then begins to change for the good. The word of God is a seed and once planted, that word takes root and begins to grow within you. The key to growing in God is by growing in the knowledge of His word.

The Adamic Nature

The Adamic nature is the nature of sin and corruption. It's this nature that we call "the old man". The old man is full of corruption, sinful habits, and desires. Paul the Apostle said, "In my flesh, dwelleth no good thing" (Romans 7:18). The flesh, which is the carnal nature of man, doesn't want change. The carnal nature loves sin. When we see so-called Christians that are hateful, full of pride, gossipers, and backbiters, these are nothing more than religious people that have not experienced true transformation.

Do not allow the carnal nature to steer the ship of your life in the wrong direction. The carnal nature will eventually lead you to destruction. As mature believers, we know what to do to maintain change. Prayer and the study of the word causes progressive change. The glory dwells in those who have learned how to conquer the carnal nature.

But until we have conquered the flesh, we

will continue to produce the fruits of the flesh. Being religious is only a formality. It's easy to look holy from the outside and have sin dwelling on the inside of you. The operations of the gifts of the spirit are not predicated on holy living. Gifts can still operate outside of holy living. Many in the body of Christ have hid behind gifts, but those who have discernment can see passed, beyond their false righteousness and charisma.

As believers we must do better and bring our flesh under subjection. When we lie or treat people vindictively, and still feel no conviction, it is a sign that we are still in the flesh. This is the reason why we must revisit the altars again. You need a personal revival to change you before God will allow you to take the spirit of revival to your generation.

This is the reason why we need a true glory encounter. The carnal nature is arrested when the glory is present. The carnal nature is forced to surrender. If you know that you have not been in your rightful place in Jesus, and have been allowing your flesh to operate, then in love, I want you to repeat after me.

Jesus restore my relationship back with you. Help me to commit myself to prayer. Give me the grace to discipline myself to study your Word. Give me a glory encounter so that I can experience true transformation and deliverance. From this day forward, help me to walk in the spirit so I will not fulfill the lust and carnal desires of my flesh. In Jesus mighty name.

Cursed Connections vs. Blessed Connections
Sometimes our transformation is hindered because we remain connected to the wrong people, places, and things in life. Paul the Apostle wrote in the NIV translation that bad company corrupts good character (see 1 Corinthians 15:33 NIV). For you to grow in the nature of Christ, you must disconnect from anything that stands as a roadblock in your life. Let me give you an example, a bad connection can be a problem and makes it

difficult to hear the other person on the line. I'm pretty sure we all have experienced bad signals and connections.

Even spiritually, a bad connection makes it hard for us to hear the voice of God. Bad connections will eventually taint your character. 2 Corinthians 6:17 says, "Wherefore come out from among them, and be ye separate, saith the Lord, and touch not the unclean thing; and I will receive you". The word *separate* in the Greek *Aphorizo* means to divide, sever, or set apart. There are some things or people that are not healthy to your spiritual life. If that connection is affecting and effecting you in a negative way, you need to sever that connection immediately.

The devil will send you delusional connections, these are connections that will appear authentic, but are sent to offset your life. Sometimes, these are people that appear positive, but their purpose and plan is to disconnect you from God. A connection is a binding or joining together. In that connection, the source of that connection gains access to you and you have access to the source, which can be good or bad.

There's also a transference of that connection, good or bad. You are influenced by that connection, good or bad. We need to discern every connection to see if it is a cursed connection or a blessed connection. Discerning the connection is important because Satan connections are cursed connections and Godly connections are blessed connections. If you join in covenant with a cursed connection, that curse then gains access to your life. You will begin to experience chaos in every area of your life. You may experience financial crisis, mental crisis or marital crisis.

A spirit of hindrance will come into your life, stopping process and everything that you do. This connection will lead you to disappointment and distress. A blessed connection is the opposite, it will give you access to the spirit of blessings and prosperity. The results in this connection will lead to happiness and Godly pleasure.

Discern Your Connections!

Glory Connections

When you are connected with the glory, you can extract what you need from the glory. Remember in Chapter 1, I talked about glory wealth. We looked at how riches are in the glory according to Philippians 4:19. Remember the word riches means money, wealth, and abundance of external possessions. External possessions are physical things.

How do you extract from the glory? First, you need to identify and discern the presence and location of the glory. This is important because the true glory of God isn't everywhere. Connect where the glory is or create your own glory environment. Principle #1 is faith. With faith, pull from the glory what you need. Principle #2 is giving. When you sow into the glory of God, God then begins to manifest the things you need from the glory.

Most of the time, when we experience a mighty move of God in our church services, we begin to feel a heavy presence of the Father's glory. But, because our expectations are so low, we leave those services without receiving anything from the Lord. Many of you discern the presence, but you didn't connect with the presence in faith and giving. The next time you encounter a heavy presence, participate in faith and giving to receive what you need.

Expectation is Principle#3. Expectation means to wait, to ask, to look out for, to envision, and to receive. When the glory shows up, you can **ask** God for what you need. Patience is required because you have to **wait** for what you ask God for from the glory. While you're in worship, in the glory, begin to **envision.** It's hard to believe what you don't see, so begin to envision what you're believing in God for from the glory.

The last definition of expectation is to receive. After waiting, asking, and seeing, **receive** what you need by faith from the glory. Receiving is key! I realize that there are so many believers that don't know how to receive. Jesus said whatsoever you shall ask in prayer, believing ye shall receive (see Matthew 21:22). In this verse, Jesus was revealing a threefold principle: asking, believing, and receiving.

Believing will prepare your heart to receive and is the first step to receiving. Receiving comes from the Greek word *Lambano* which means to take or catch. Some things you have to take in the spirit and other things you have to catch in the spirit. Faith, giving, and expectation applied together are how to receive what you need out of the glory.

Righteous Transformation

The power of glory will transform you to become righteous before the Lord. Righteousness is something that God the

Father desires to see in all of His children for God is righteous (see 2 Chronicles 12:6).

Righteousness is an attribute of God, so when we put on righteousness, we become like our Father God. Righteousness is a very important subject because the glory will always come to a people that's full of the spirit of righteousness.

Not to say that sinners cannot experience the glory of God, but the glory will be revealed to a sinner that's hungry and desperate for God and change. I believe in the last days, we will see a mass remnant of ungodly men and women transformed by the power of God. The spirit of repentance and conviction will fall upon them. 2 Corinthians 7:10 says, "Godly sorrow brings repentance that leads to salvation and leaves no regret, but worldly sorrow brings death..." (NIV).

Their eyes will become open to the truth of Jesus Christ and righteousness will become their pursuit. Righteousness simply means to be in right standing with God. Righteousness has nothing to do with you being perfect. God is not looking for perfection from you, God is looking for maturity in you. If you could live a perfect life, we wouldn't need Jesus. So, because of our imperfection, Jesus died for us so God could see the perfection and righteousness of Jesus in you.

We are righteous by faith according to Romans 9:30, "What shall we say then? That the Gentiles, which followed not after righteousness, have attained to righteousness, even the righteousness which is of faith."

The Bible says that Abraham believed God, and it was counted unto him for righteousness (see Romans 4:3). Righteousness means for those that have been redeemed by the blood of Jesus Christ, that when God sees you, He sees the righteousness, holiness, and innocence of Jesus Christ in you.

The reason I'm discussing righteousness is

because many believers in Christ want to demonstrate the power of Christ without obeying kingdom standards. Righteousness is a standard that we are to uphold. Even though righteousness is by faith, love, obedience, and good works are things God looks to see in our actions towards others. When we leave this earth one day, God is going to judge our actions.

After becoming righteous, before the Lord by faith, we must practice the righteous acts of God (see 1 Samuel 12:7). I believe that God desires to release His glory to this generation, but the spirit of righteousness must be restored. Where there's righteousness, there will be glory. The Bible says that God is in the generation of the righteous (see Psalm 14:5).

If God can be in a generation, this also means that God can be out of a generation. A generation without God is scary. This means much calamity, disaster, and destruction. We must pray that God restores righteousness to our generation. When the righteous come together to pray, God's hand will begin to move upon our nation in a powerful way. We will see political, economic, and judicial changes for the better.

I said judicial because many judicial laws have been created that do not coincide with the laws of God. Proverbs 14:12 tells us, "There is a way which seemeth right unto a man, but the end thereof are the ways of death." There are many things that people do that appear right, but isn't right according to the Word of God. God isn't going to compromise His righteousness so why should we? The cry out of a heart of righteousness will attract God's attention towards you. A heart of righteousness will move God to bring great deliverance (see Psalms 34:18).

Nowadays, when we enforce the term righteousness, we are accused of being legalistic but the truth is many don't want to let their personal sins go. God will turn His face from sin and place His eyes upon the righteous (see 1 Peter 3:12). In the Old Testament, the priest offered animal sacrifices, but for new covenant believers, God is looking for a sacrifice of righteousness (see Psalm 4:5). You must destroy your carnal nature in order for the righteousness of God to live in you.

King David did not say to offer the sacrifice of religion, he said to offer the sacrifice of righteousness. We must learn to guard and protect our righteousness. It is the devil's job to steal our righteousness (see John 10:10). Once we've learned to keep our righteousness by telling sin no, glory access will be available to us.

Holy Transformation
Holiness is another word that many shun from due to the lifestyle that holiness requires. Holiness is not to be overlooked. It will prepare you to experience the presence and glory of God. I find that it is possible to be religious and not be holy. Just because you

practice religion or have a formality of godliness doesn't mean you're saved or holy.

My heart's desire is to restore the significance of holiness back to the body of Christ. Beautiful singing, prolific preaching, and high praise and dancing means nothing to God if it's not coming from a person that's walking in true holiness. God's not moved by church theatrics, he's moved by the believer that embraces holiness. Holiness is a requirement to see God and without it you will never see him. Hebrews 12:14 assures us, "Follow peace with all men, and holiness, without which no man shall see the Lord."

Holiness comes from the Greek word *hagiasmos* which means sanctification of heart and life. Holiness is when you sanctify your heart so that your life can reflect the light of Jesus Christ. That light can be His love, meekness, and compassion. Holiness speaks of God's divine nature and is the attribute of God that Jesus displayed while living on earth.

Let me give you another powerful definition of holiness. Holiness means to be separated from sin and to be consecrated to God. Paul the Apostle said, "in my flesh dwelleth no good thing..." (see Romans 7:18). In the carnal nature, there are things that war against the righteousness and holiness of God. Sin can be tempting to the flesh that's not crucified and is transgressing against the laws of God.

Sin will keep you separated from God and all of heaven's blessings for you on earth. Holiness is the nature of the new man and the new man is the renewed man. The new man is the crucified and Christ man. To put on the new man is to put on holiness. Ephesians 4:24 reminds us, "And that ye put on the new man, which after God is created in righteousness and true holiness."

In the Old Testament, the priests were to wear holy garments (see Exodus 29:29). If we're not careful, the sins of this world will put dirt on our spiritual garments. Anything that's dirty needs to be washed. Do not allow the devil to trick you into being religiously dirty. The devil doesn't mind you going forth in your ministry as long as your life is dirty with the sins of this world.

There are many in the body of Christ who need to purify their dirty garments. Once true holiness comes back to the church, the glory of God will follow. God is seeking for holy people to tabernacle his glory in. The glory of God rested in the holy Ark of the Covenant. If you notice, I said *holy* ark (see 2 Chronicles 35:3). Like the ark, when you become holy, the glory will rest in you too.

The priests were permitted to eat the shewbread or the bread of presence in the holy place (see Leviticus 6:16). The priests were also permitted to eat the sin offering, which was most holy in the holy place (see Leviticus 6:23 - 26). My point is that you must become a holy and consecrated priest. You must enter the holy place in order to receive spiritual food which is revelations and secrets from God.

All throughout the Bible the word holy is mentioned:

• Holy angels (see Matthew 25:31) - theophanic messengers were created to serve God and mankind.

• Holy anointed oil (see Exodus 30:31) - a substance used for consecrating the chosen person.

• Holy mountain of God (see Ezekiel 8:14) - a high place where God's prophet would go to meet with God.

• Holy prophets (see 2 Peter 3:2) - prophetic messengers sent to bring direction and prophetic revelation.

• Holy apostles (see Ephesians 3:5) - apostolic messengers sent to establish the doctrine of Christ and apostolic revelation.

• Holy garments (see Exodus 29:29) - represents a pure and holy lifestyle, uncontaminated by the world.

- Holy burnt offering (see Leviticus 6:26) - what we offer to God: praise, singing, worship, out of a pure heart, mind and soul.
- God's name is holy (see Leviticus 22:2) - we should never profane the name of God.
- Holy vessels (see 1 Kings 8:4, 2 Timothy 2:20) - metaphorically we are called to be holy vessels, containers of the presence of God.
- Holy Ark of the Covenant (see 2 Chronicles 35:3) - a holy box that represented the glory of God.
- Holy Spirit (see Acts 1:8) - the spirit of God given to the church as both gift and promise.

As a priestly people, living holy is key to accessing the glory of God.

CHAPTER 6

The God Man

B efore I begin this chapter, I want to clarify that when I titled this portion of the chapter, the God Man, I was also referring to woman as the God Man. In the scriptures, God also sees women as sons spiritually (see Romans 8:14). In the book of Genesis, Adam was the first God Man on earth (see Genesis 1:26 and Genesis 2:7). When God formed man of the dust, God breathed Himself into Adam's nostrils the breath of life. God then began living inside of man.

Adam began to operate in power, authority, and dominion on earth. God made man king of the earth. God sat on his throne in heaven and watched man rule on earth like God the Father rules in heaven. In the New Testament, Jesus Christ was also *theos anthropos* which means the God Man. *Theos* in the Greek means God, *anthropos* in the Greek means man.

When Jesus lived on earth, the power of His father moved through Him. How was Jesus able to operate in this supernatural power? Simple. Jesus submitted to the instructions of God His father that lived in Him. Jesus understood that God is the source to miraculous power. When Jesus submitted to God as the source, miraculous power became available to Him. He learned to submit and obey His Father's commands. Jesus Christ only spoke what God had commanded Him (see John 12:49).

Through obedience, Jesus Christ gained

access to the Father's power. As God's children, as we grow in obedience, we grow in the power of God. Obedience was key to Jesus' power. Paul the Apostle said that Jesus was obedient unto death, even the death of the cross (see Philippians 2:8). Jesus mastered obedience. We master obedience when we fully obey and follow God's instructions.

As Adam was a God Man, and Jesus was a God Man, now God wants to raise up another God Man in you, to share in power with God. As a God Man the power of God is part of your inheritance. So, why is it that many that are sons of God are not operating in the power of God? God is very wise. He knows our level of maturity as sons. God isn't going to give great power to someone that is simple minded and immature.

God gives His power in measures. The level of power God gives you is based on your level of maturity and sacrifice. It is foolish and immature to seek for power and not seek and love the giver of that power. A God Man is full grown and mature spiritually. Be a God Man and not a God boy. A God boy is one who has God but isn't fully mature in God.

Paul the Apostle emphasized that the purpose of the 5-fold ministry was to equip the Body of Christ to becoming a mature man. Ephesians 4:13 states, "Till we all come in the unity of the faith, and of the knowledge of the Son of God, unto a perfect man, unto the measure of the stature of the fullness of Christ."

Paul the Apostle desired to see the church come into a perfect man meaning a mature church. *Perfect* in the Greek *teleios* means full grown, adult, mature, and man. God wants us to become a full grown, mature man in the spiritual. Remember I'm talking about women too. Boy is defined as an immature male. In the early stages of our walk with God, we made a lot of mistakes due to being immature. There are others that have been saved for a while and they are still making the same immature mistakes.

Sometimes, we justify these mistakes so we
can remain in an immature mindset. I say
this in love. It's just time to grow up so that
we can grow in power with God. Paul the
Apostle wrote to the Corinthian church
concerning the envy, strife, and division that
was going on in the church (see 1 Corinthians
13:1-3). Paul called them babes in Christ. He
didn't say full grown in Christ. *Babe* in the
Greek *neplou* means childish, untaught, and
unskilled and figuratively speaking, it means
immature Christians.

Paul the Apostle was addressing them as
immature Christians. You will never expand
in God's glory and power as long as you
remain immature. Paul looked at them as
worldly believers in the church. Have you
ever wondered how God sees you? Does
God see you as mature or immature? The
Corinthian church was full of envy, strife, and
division. This type of behavior will hinder the
glory and power of God from flowing in your

life.

I want you to take notice that there's a difference between power and glory. My reasoning for explaining this is that God doesn't just want His power to flow through you, God wants His glory to flow through you too. *Power* in the Greek *dunamis* means miraculous power. This is the power that comes from the Holy Spirit through fasting and praying. This power is called the anointing.

Glory is the power of God that's much greater, stronger, mightier, and effective than the anointing. God desires for His glory to flow through you, not just His gifts and anointings. Both terms are the power of God, just on different levels. I know that in these last days, the end time remnant is not only going to operate in the anointing, we are going to see the remnant operating in the glory realm. As a God Man, you are called to operate in the glory realm.

God Lives in the God Man

Jesus Christ the God Man was a very humble, compassionate and loving. Through His examples the secrets to the power of God were revealed. We must study the life of Jesus to discover His relationship with God. His relationship with God was so intimate. When your relationship with God becomes your focus, everything else becomes secondary. God the Father becomes number one above everything else.

This is the attitude that Christ had with God His father. Not only did Jesus have a powerful, intimate relationship with God the Father, but the Father also lived in Him. One day, Philip the Apostle asked Jesus to show him the Father. Philip the Apostle was speaking about God (see John 14:8). Jesus responded and said, "He that hath seen me hath seen the Father..." (see John 14:9).

In verse 10, Jesus revealed that the Father lived in Him (see John 14:10). God is looking for earthly tabernacles, bodies He can live in. The secret to operating in the same anointing that Christ walked in is by yielding, submitting, and obeying the Christ that's in you. Jesus said, "no man cometh unto the Father, but by me..." (see John 14:6). This means you cannot access God or His glory without going through Jesus Christ.

God lived behind the veil of Christ's flesh as stated in Hebrews 10:20, "By a new and living way, which he hath consecrated for us, through the veil, that is to say, his flesh." This is the reason why Jesus had to go through a crucifying process. So, that we could go beyond the veil of his flesh to get to God. I'm so happy that through Jesus obedience and crucifying the veil of His flesh, we gain access back to God.

Jesus and God are one according to the scriptures (see John 10:30). When we look at God the Father, Son and Holy Spirit, all three are one, just three manifestations of God. Jesus is His own person, the Holy

Spirit is His own person, but both are one with God. Jesus said, "for my Father is greater than I..." (see John 14:28) which means that Jesus was serving someone that was greater than Himself.

Paul the Apostle revealed that God knows the mind of the spirit (see Romans 8:27) which means that God has a mind and the Holy Spirit has a mind, but they are one. What I want you to understand is that God Himself wants to live in you. Not just Jesus and the Holy Spirit. Paul the Apostle said to the church of Ephesians to be followers of God as dear children (see Ephesians 5:1).

Followers in the Greek *mimetes* means imitator. As believers we are called to imitate God on earth (see Ephesians 5:1). In 1 Corinthians 11:1 (NLT), Paul the Apostle was an imitator of Christ. One verse tells us to be imitators of God and the other verse an imitator of Christ.

Here's the revelation: when we imitate Christ,

we move in the realm of anointing. Christ literally means the anointed one. When we imitate God, we move in the realm of glory. We have to imitate Christ before we can imitate God the Father.

You will learn the nature of God as you imitate Jesus Christ. The Bible says that God and Jesus are equal (see John 5:18 and Philippians 2:6). The word *equal* in the Greek *isos* means agree together. Jesus is always in agreement with the Father. The first step to imitating God is by first imitating Christ. The Christ relationship will teach you how to operate in the anointing and glory realm.

As we strive to master imitating Christ, Jesus will then begin to teach us how to operate in the glory realm of the Father. Jesus came in His Father's name (see John 5:43) which means that He was operating in His father's authority. This same power and authority is available to you only when you submit to the divinity meaning the God inside of you. Paul the Apostle shared a very powerful revelation to the Ephesian church on how to be filled with all the fullness of God (see Ephesians 3:19).

When I read this years ago, I was surprised that it is possible to be filled with all the fullness of God. The word *filled* in the Greek *pleroo* means fill up, fill to the brim, and increase. As believers, God wants us to be filled with all the fullness of Him. Paul the Apostle revealed a powerful key in his writing on how to increase God in you and that key is love (see Ephesians 3:17).

Love Unlocks the Fullness of God in You

Ephesians 3:17-18 says, "That Christ may dwell in your hearts by faith; that ye, being rooted and grounded in love, May be able to comprehend with all saints what is the breadth, and length, and depth, and height."

Paul the Apostle was explaining to the Ephesian church that there's dimensions to God's love. One word that he used in describing God's love is depth. *Depth* in the Greek *bathos* means mystery or deep things of God. Love is the key that gives us access to the mysteries of God. If you desire to come into glory revelation, begin to operate in God's love.

Love is the key to being filled with all the fullness of God on earth. God is multidimensional, so when you operate in His love, other dimensions of God are open to you. Let me give you a few of these dimensions: God's love, God's power, God's grace, God's glory, God's anointings, and God's presence. God and love are inseparable so to grow in love is to grow in God. Love is the greatest secret to the power of God.

Fasting and prayer will not release the power of God in your life until love is applied. If you're fasting without love you're just starving yourself. You cannot fast and pray and still speak negative about people and still expect God to honor your sacrifice Proverbs 15:8

says, "The sacrifice of the wicked is an abomination to the LORD: but the prayer of the upright is His delight."

Before we talk about the gifts of the spirit and miracles, signs, and wonders, let us first practice loving one another. Love is the greatest gift and Jesus was that gift! Jesus is God and God is love. It breaks my heart when I see Christians mistreating people such as: looking down on the poor, abusing our authority in the church, slandering each other's character, or not being apologetic after wronging someone. This isn't Christlike.

Where is our conviction, our repentance? When we minister to others the love of Jesus, it gives Jesus an opportunity to touch them. Jesus operates through love. Love was Jesus' greatest asset and through this asset God was able to touch the world. Jesus preached, taught, prophesied, healed, delivered, and performed miracles out of love.

Love is the vehicle that God uses to channel

Himself through. As the body of Christ returns to the love of God, the world then will experience the fullness of God. Yes, God is going to come back for a glorious church, but a glorious church is a church full of love. I want to give you 4 dimensions of love. First, *agape* which is the love of God. Secondly, *eros* which is romantic love. Next is *philadelphia*, which is brotherly love. Fourthly, *phileo* which is the friendship type of love.

But the greatest of the four is agape love. This love isn't based on condition. If you're not romantic with Jesus, He will still agape you. If you are not showing forth brotherly love, Jesus will still agape you. If you are not showing forth friendship, Jesus will yet agape you. Again, the agape love isn't based on how good, righteous, or holy you are.

This is the love we must master in our walk with God. To understand agape love is to understand God. To study agape love is to study God. To experience agape love is to experience God. To feel agape love is to feel God. Agape love is very strong and powerful and can be felt in a tangible way.

For example. When you feel the presence of God, you are experiencing God's love towards you. Can you imagine when we get to heaven and experience the power of the Father's love for all of eternity? Jesus was able to practice the love of God daily because he remained intimate with the God that lived in Him. Colossians 2:9 confirms, "For in him dwelleth all the fullness of the Godhead bodily..." (also see Colossians 1:19).

Godhead in the Greek *theotes* means divinity. Through agape love, Jesus was extraordinary and supernatural and was able to operate from His divine nature. Loving your enemy is a true sign that God's love is in your heart. Jesus tells us to love our enemies (see Matthew 5:44). Loving a friend isn't complicated but loving an enemy is complicated when you try loving them in the flesh. This is the reason why we need the

Holy Spirit. The Holy Spirit fills our heart with the love of Jesus Christ (see Romans 5:5).

The Holy Spirit will empower you to love the way God loves. When you have learned to overcome hate by forgiving your enemies, then are you ready for power. When Jesus was on the cross, He tells God to forgive them for they know not what they do (see Luke 23:34). This is very powerful because Jesus knew how to love beyond His pain.

Many of you have been hurt by enemies but can you still love them despite the hurt they caused you? This is true love. Can you love beyond offense? Can you love beyond the fact that you've been let down or forsaken by people you trusted? This is the love that God wants us to grow in. This level of love will unlock the power and glory of God in you.

This level of love will cause God to be filled up in you. The Bible says that God is love (see 1 John 4:8) which means that love is a person. This is the reason why agape love can be felt in a tangible way when we encounter His presence. God's presence is His love. That love came to earth in the person of Jesus Christ. There's so much we can discuss about the love of God but my point in sharing this is that love is the key to experiencing God increasing in you.

CHAPTER 7

The Spirit of God

The Holy Spirit is the precious spirit of God. The Holy Spirit was both gift and promise to the body of Christ. The Holy Spirit was sent to earth to empower the believer to walk in the character of Christ. Without the Holy Spirit, we will be powerless Christians. The church doesn't speak much about the Holy Spirit, but I know that if we embrace the purpose and ministry of the spirit, we would see more manifestations of the spirit.

I want to talk about a few manifestations of the spirit. The Holy Spirit can manifest in the form of gifts, fruit, and power. The manifestation of the Holy Spirit are His gifts such as: word of wisdom, word of knowledge, faith, gifts of healing, working of miracles, prophecy, discerning of spirits, diverse kinds of tongues, and interpretation of tongues (see 1 Corinthians 12:8-10).

The Holy Spirit will also manifest 9 fruits which is His characteristics which is love, joy, peace, longsuffering, gentleness, goodness, faith, meekness, and temperance (see Galatians 5:22). The Holy Spirit can also manifest in miraculous power Acts 1:8, "But ye shall receive power, after that the Holy Ghost is come upon you: and ye shall be witnesses unto me both in Jerusalem, and in all Judaea, and in Samaria, and unto the uttermost part of the earth". For those who have never received the baptism of the Holy Spirit, this supernatural gift is available to you.

Once you've received this precious gift, you will begin to manifest His gifts, fruit, power, and receive new heavenly language in you. I remember years ago when I first received the baptism of the Holy Spirit. It was an amazing experience. At the time I was living in my home city, Springfield, Illinois. Before I share my experience with the Holy Spirit, I want to share a little bit about my past with you before my conversion.

I was a young, 17-year-old drug dealer that was on my way to hell. One day an old friend of mine and I were sitting on my front porch selling drugs. Two undercover cops came pretending to buy drugs. I jumped up to get the sale before my friend and was getting ready to invite the undercover cops into my home. Suddenly, I hear the words, "You're under arrest."

Slammed to the ground and handcuffed, I was busted. I was then taken to the county jail for questioning. Because this was my first recorded offense, I was given two years of probation and then released. My girlfriend at the time and I moved in with a Christian lady that was saved. This precious lady told me that there was something special about me and invited me to her church.

I remember going to this church, and they that were believers were speaking in this strange language. I knew nothing about the Holy Spirit and speaking in tongues. All I knew was that I wanted what they had. My pastor at the time scheduled for the saints to meet weekly on Wednesdays at 7:00 or 8:00pm. I went to prayer one Wednesday night and I entered the double doors to enter the sanctuary, the sounds of different languages were coming out of the mouths of those that were praying.

I went to my pastor and told him that I wanted to speak in tongues. He took me to the mid-section of the sanctuary and we kneeled together. He had me to read a

couple of scriptures about the Holy Spirit
and then laid his hands on me and suddenly,
I began to speak in this new heavenly
language. It felt like electricity was moving
throughout my body.

What an experience this was for me! After
the encounter, I supernaturally began to
forgive and love people effortlessly. If you're
reading this book and desire to be saved and
filled with the Holy Spirit, repeat after me.

*Lord Jesus I confess that I am a sinner. I
believe you died for my sins. I open my heart
to you now and I receive you into my life as
my Lord and savior (see Romans 10:9).*

Now say: *Lord fill me with the Holy Spirit so
that I can demonstrate the same love and
power on earth as you did in Jesus mighty
name. Amen.*

There are many attributes and characteristics
of the Holy Spirit but Peter the Apostle
refers to the Holy Spirit as the Spirit of Glory

(see 1 Peter 4:14). Not only will the Holy Spirit manifest truth, grace, and holiness, but the Holy Spirit will manifest glory. As He is the spirit of glory, He wants to manifest glory through you. This is why it's so important to commune with the Holy Spirit. He is to teach us about the ways of God. You will never flow in the glory of the spirit if you don't know the ways of God.

The Holy Spirit wants to be a gentle friend to many of you. We must learn to get in a quiet place of meditation every day to hear what the spirit has to say. The Bible says the Holy Spirit speaks what He hears (see John 16:13). He will reveal things to you concerning your future. You will never get to your future if you never make time for the Holy Spirit to speak to you about your future.

There are so many Christians that have become insensitive to the presence of the Holy Spirit. As a result, the Holy Spirit is speaking but we cannot hear Him. The Holy Spirit is giving wisdom, counsel, and revelation, but we are too carnal to hear His voice. The Holy Spirit spoke in the New Testament to Barnabas and Saul who later became Paul (see Acts 13:2). The Holy Spirit is still speaking today.

He desires to speak to you about your purpose in life. He wants to reveal more about Jesus Christ to you but if He is rejected by you how can he then minister these things to you? The Holy Spirit or the spirit of glory becomes grieved when we disobey His voice.

For those that know the Holy Spirit, but have rejected Him, I want to reintroduce you back to Him. For those who have never met the Holy Spirit, now is your opportunity to get to know Him. In your spare time, I want you to study pneumatology, which is the study of the Holy Spirit.

The Holy Spirit inspired the prophets and apostles, and He is still inspiring believers today. 2 Timothy 3:16-17 states, "All scripture is given by inspiration of God, and is profitable for doctrine, for reproof, for correction, for instruction in righteousness: That the man of God may be perfect, thoroughly furnished unto all good works."

Inspired in the Greek *theopneustos* means divinely breathed. God wants to divinely breathe the breath of His Spirit into many of those who have never been filled. I believe that God is going to breathe His Spirit upon this generation in a mighty way. A mighty outpouring of God's Spirit is coming to earth even greater than what we read in Acts 2 on the day of Pentecost.

We need the Holy Spirit to do the work of the ministry with power and demonstration. It's time to get busy doing the work of the Lord by the leading of the Holy Spirit. We are in the dispensation of the Holy Spirit and it's time to see Him fully manifesting His ministry on earth. The Holy Spirit has work to do but false religious systems have kept Him suppressed.

We grieve the spirit of God on so many levels and we don't even recognize it. We spend a lot of time trying to discern the sins of people rather than discerning the mind of the spirit. The fellowship of the spirit is a key to the power and glory of God. He wants to reveal glory revelation to those who are willing to commune with Him.

When you learn the character of the spirit, we develop a God perspective. We see people the way God sees them. God want us to see the world out of the eyes of love. Love will help the Holy Spirit to perform His ministry and anointing through you. The Holy Spirit not only wants to manifest the anointing through you, He's also ready to manifest the glory through you, as He is the spirit of glory.

As we follow the leadership of the Holy Spirit, He's going to bring us into the place of destination. Paul the Apostle said for as many as are led by the Spirit of God, they are the sons of God (See Romans 8:14)". *Led* in the

Greek *ago* means to bring to the point of destination. The Holy Spirit has knowledge of the path that we are to take in life.

So, we must learn to fully submit to His instructions when He speaks. Submission comes from a Latin word *submissionem* which means humble obedience. Humility and obedience is what God is looking for from His children. The prefix in the word submission "sub" means under. God wants us to submit under the influence and power of the Holy Spirit.

There are laws in the Holy Spirit. Paul the Apostle said the law of the spirit of life in Christ Jesus have made me free from the law of sin and death (see Romans 8:2). The laws of the spirit are principles that govern the new nature. When we break His laws or rules, the Holy Spirit becomes grieved. Yes, the Holy Spirit has feelings. Miracles and breakthroughs happen when we honor and respect the Holy Spirit.

The Holy Spirit is precious and He is to be valued for He's the presence and power of God. When God creates He speaks a word and the power of the Spirit begins to manifest that word that was spoken out of the mouth of God. From the beginning of time, before all creation, the Holy Spirit existed (see Genesis 1:2).

The Holy Spirit was the power behind everything God has spoken or created. What a privilege to have the same person, presence, and power living in you! The Holy Spirit knows the Father, so let Him teach you about Him. The Holy Spirit knows Jesus so let Him teach you about Him. The Holy Spirit knows you so let Him help you find your identity in Christ Jesus. The Holy Spirit is a master teacher, He knows the Bible better than we do. So, let Him guide you through the scriptures, as He enlightens the eyes of your understanding. It's not enough to know the logos word. It's possible to know the logos word of God without understanding. That's why receiving a Rhema word is important. Because a Rhema word comes when we read the word of God with understanding and revelation. This is the reason why we need the Holy Spirit.

He is the Spirit of Revelation (Ephesians 1:17). John the Apostle said, "I was in the spirit on the Lord's Day..." (see Revelations 1:10). John the Apostle was in the spirit but he received the revelation of the end times. As the revelation of Jesus Christ was being unfolded to him, he saw the Antichrist, the seven angels, the Seven Seals that were open, the seven trumpets that were blown, and the seven plagues that were released upon the Earth. He saw the Great Tribulation.

He saw all this things in the spirit. God is no respecter of person. You're just as significant as John the Apostle. God wants to show you a great Revelation through His Spirit too. In the last days, we are going to come into revelations from the spirit through prophetic dreams and visions that we have never heard or seen.

These Revelations have been preserved for the final dispensation. This is why the Holy Spirit is getting the church ready now. Jesus is soon to return. We must prepare ourselves for a great Spiritual Awakening and the Holy Spirit is going to play a big part in the last days.

The Holy Spirit is going to manifest a greater level of his presence, power, love, and Glory. I tell you that many prophecies will be fulfilled by the ministry of the Holy Spirit and working of angels. I'm so excited about this great news and thankful the Holy Spirit that has inspired me to write in this book. Paul the Apostle said walk in the spirit so we will not feel the lust of the flesh.

Walk, in the Greek *peripateo,* means to live. We are called to live in the realm of the spirit. This means that we should operate from this eternal realm. In this realm, you will see, hear and feel spiritual activities both good and evil. This realm will open your eyes to revelations beyond the earth realm. This is part of the ministry of the Holy Spirit. Remember the Holy Spirit is key to unlocking the glory in you.

CHAPTER 8

The Visitations

In this chapter, I want to share with you powerful visitations from the Lord that I've had from childhood to adulthood. I'm pretty sure that many of you have had visitations from the Lord too. Supernatural visitations occur throughout the Bible, from the Old Testament to the New Testament. I'm going to share my visitation experiences in this book and then give you scriptural reference to show you that visitations from the Lord are biblical.

I believe the Lord wants us to experience a

lifetime of visitations on earth. Many characters in the Bible receive multiple visitations from the Lord. Most of the time, visitations occur unexpectedly. In this chapter, I want to explain the importance of visitations. To experience visitations is part of living a supernatural life. My prayer is as you read this chapter, God gives you powerful, supernatural visitations.

Sometimes, God wants to speak to you through visitations or impart something to you, such as a spiritual gift, anointings, and mantles. Sometimes God will give you a prophecy or allow you to experience a strong presence. In a visitation, you may feel the presence of an angel or even Jesus. In a visitation you may see an angel or see the risen Savior Jesus Christ appear to you.

All visitations aren't the same. You can have a visitation from the Lord while sleeping or awake. A visitation is defined as the appearance or coming of a supernatural influence or spirit. If you see an angel or

Jesus appear to you, don't be afraid. By the way, when they appear, fear automatically leaves when the power of peace is present.

Jesus Visitation

I remember one early morning, I woke up in a trance. This has happened to me many times, but I noticed that this trance experience was different. I recognized a man in a robe, standing on the left side of my bed. In my mind, I'm thinking what is Jesus doing in my room. I remember as I was attempting to get up out of the bed, I noticed that there was another supernatural entity also in my room.

To my knowledge, it was an angel after seeing his white wing. Jesus never said anything to me, he just looked at me. When the visitation had ended, I was shocked that Christ had appeared in my room. I called this married couple that I knew and told them what had happened to me. They were amazed and excited about my experience. When I ended the call, I fell on my knees at the side of my bed and I began weeping uncontrollably before the Lord. In this visitation, I saw Jesus manifest before me.

Another time I had a night vision and I saw Jesus in the sky, standing in the clouds. I noticed that He was not dressed in His traditional white robe. He was dressed in gold armor with a large gold sword on His side. Jesus said, "I came not to bring peace but a sword..." (see Matthew 10:34). I tell you the truth, Jesus looked awesome! The gold that I saw was not of this earth and didn't look like 10 or 14 carat gold. I knew it was a divine gold or a gold that only existed in heaven.

As I was looking at Jesus in the sky, it appeared as if He was getting ready to come to earth to fight in battle. There was one thing that was missing in this night vision or dream, and that was I couldn't see His face. So, when I awakened, I asked God, why He didn't allow me to see the face of Jesus. I went into prayer, asking God to show me the face of Jesus.

I want to say I sought God for 6 or 7 days to grant my request. Finally, God answered my prayers. One particular morning, I woke up, and guess what? The beautiful face of Jesus was right in front of me. I didn't see His body, only His beautiful face.

Another time, I was in the spirit, talking with God and Jesus at the same time. Suddenly, I saw a box with a ribbon on top of it descending from heaven. In this visitation, Jesus was giving me a gift. Sometimes, gifts can be imparted in a visitation. In the last days, many unbelievers will be visited by Jesus, many will be converted by these Jesus visitations. Many Muslims have been saved by Jesus after seeing Jesus in a dream, vision, or in physical manifestation.

In the Bible, Jesus appeared to many people after His death, burial, and resurrection. Jesus appeared to Mary Magdalene (see John 20:14-16). Jesus appeared to Peter (see Luke

24:34) and to two disciples (Luke 24:13-16).
Jesus appeared to His 11 disciples (see
Matthew 28:16-17) and also to Thomas (see
John 20:24-29). Jesus appeared to about 500
people (see 1 Corinthians 15:6).

Angelic Visitations

One early morning, I saw in the spirit and an
angel came into my room. At first, I didn't
know what the angel was because it appeared
as a small ball of light. As this ball of light
floated towards me, the ball of light began to
grow bigger and bigger. As this glorious ball
of light stood in front of me, I saw these
bright hands extend from this glorious light
and enter my stomach.

I didn't feel any pain at all, then the angel
flew away. I knew that the angel of the Lord
had given me an impartation. Angels can give
impartations (see Ezekiel 3:1-2). In another
supernatural experience, I was in a night
vision, and I saw a beautiful white horse with
wings running west in the clouds (see
Zachariah 6:3). As this beautiful white horse

was running, I saw a huge white angel with huge white wings, manifest out of the clouds.

When I saw the angel, I realized that I was in a vision. Angels can appear to people as one did to Moses (see Exodus 3:2). An angel appeared to Gideon (see Judges 6:12). Angels have a ministry. When God has given you a kingdom assignment, God assigns angels to assist you. Hebrews 1:14 says, "Are they not all ministering spirits, sent forth to minister for them who shall be heirs of salvation?"

Angels can even appear in a dream just like with Joseph (see Matthew 1:20). Angels can also appear in visions (see Ezekiel Chapter 1 and 10). The Bible is full of scriptures that reference angelic visitations. If you have never seen an angel, ask God the Father to reveal angels to you. Many think that angelic manifestations were only for those in the Bible.

Listen - that is religious, erroneous teaching.

One time, I had a dream of angels right after I asked God to show me angels. People will tell you that it is wrong to ask God for the deeper things of the spirit, but those type of people have a shallow relationship with God. The Holy Spirit wants to take you deeper in God, so get ready for angelic visitations.

Demonic Visitations

Decades ago, I was probably 4 or 5 years old, when Satan appeared to me. I will never forget this terrifying experience. At the time my sister had a purple big wheel. You know this was many years ago, I don't know if they even make big wheels anymore. I was outside in the front yard and there was a young girl, probably also my age, talking about the devil.

I remember opening my mouth and saying, "I'm not scared of the devil." After that, we ended the discussion. I decided to sit down on the purple big wheel and something told me to look up. As I looked up, I saw Satan laughing at me. He was standing in midair, in a transparent form; I was able to look right through him. Fear and terror gripped me, and I took off running, screaming. This was my first demonic encounter with the devil.

There was another time I was walking with my cousins to their sister's house to play video games. I was probably around 13 years old. As we were on our way, I heard a demonic voice in my ears. This demonic spirit started by laughing at me, then began speaking with me. I didn't know if this was the devil or a demon spirit. I heard this voice audible in my ears. My cousins and my brother didn't hear what I heard. Once again, I was terrified.

Another satanic vision occurred in the form of a night vision. In this vision, I was standing in the middle of a desert, and saw Satan about a mile away from where I was standing. My eyes supernaturally zoomed in to see him. I saw Satan looking into the heavens, roaring at God. I tell you that Satan was extremely angry. In this vision it was like his roar went throughout the whole world (see 1

Peter 5:8). That's how powerful his roar was. But we know Satan's power doesn't stand a chance against the power of God, Hallelujah.

Another time, I had an open vision and I was in my bedroom and I saw what looked like a flat screen television above my bedroom door. In this vision I saw Satan sitting on a throne and he had big black horns coming out of both sides of his head. He looked like a bodybuilder and I saw extreme darkness in his eyes.

He looked at me with anger in his face and I can still remember this vision as if it were yesterday. Then, suddenly, the vision vanished. Can demons appear in dreams? Absolutely! I've been attacked by demons in my dreams and have had more demonic encounters but I've decided to mention these few.

Don't allow these demonic visitations to frighten you. You have power through Jesus Christ to conquer demons. For a long time, I didn't understand why Satan came to me, but now I know he wanted to destroy me. As a spirit, he saw that I had a great purpose over my life and he knew my purpose was to destroy his kingdom.

This explains the reason why some of you have had demonic experiences. The devil was after you. He saw the hand of God on your life. The devil doesn't play fair and he will try everything in his power to destroy you, but the born again in Christ Jesus are covered by His blood. The purpose for demonic visitations is to pull you away from God. That's why children, most of the time, have demonic experiences at a young age.

Glory Visitation

I shared with you a few of the visitations that I've had and I believe that some of you will be able to relate to my experiences. Your visitations are to be shared as a tool for evangelism. Your visitations are a part of your testimony. Some share their visitations to sound deep and to be look upon as some great wonder.

This type of attitude reveals the spirit of pride. For this reason, God put a thorn in Paul's flesh to keep him humble. 2 Corinthians 12:7 says, "And lest I should be exalted above measure through the abundance of the revelations, there was given to me a thorn in the flesh, the messenger of Satan to buffet me, lest I should be exalted above measure."

Being super spiritual doesn't make you great. God exalts the humble not the proud. Share your divine encounters in the spirit of humility. Share them on social media, share them with friends and family, and share them with the world. God has given you these visitations for a reason, so share your experiences with boldness and confidence.

For those who have never had a divine encounter, this doesn't mean you're not special. Begin to ask God for a visitation, He will give you one. God desires to expose you to the supernatural but there must be a desire for it. I want you all to know that there is a mighty move of God that is near. The world will experience a glory visitation on earth.

I'm excited to be living in this dispensation of time. I know that Jesus is on His way back. You cannot afford to allow the spirit of pride to cause you to miss this next move of God or glory visitation. Pride is a demonic spirit that has grown strong in our world today but it is a spirit that must be conquered. Pride will hinder you from experiencing the glory of God.

Pride is a dangerous spirit and a spirit that God hates. It's a spirit that God rejects. It's a spirit that God despises. You will never be great in God if the spirit of pride is sitting on the throne of your heart. The scripture says pride goeth before destruction and a haughty spirit before a fall (see Proverbs 16:18). The Bible says that pride shall bring a man low, but honor shall uphold the humble in spirit (see Proverbs 29:23).

The Bible says the Lord hates a proud look (see Proverbs 6:16). This verse reveals that God hates a proud look. The word hate in the Hebrew *sane* means to turn against. So, if pride is in you, God is going to turn against you.

As we look at the character of Christ, His personality did not reflect pride. Jesus was meek and lowly, meek meaning gentle and lowly meaning humble. There was no pride in Him. So, to be Christlike means to shun from things that do not reflect His character, such as pride. The Bible says God hears the desires of the humble (see Psalms 10:17).

So, the opposite is that God doesn't hear the heart of the proud. Pride will hinder you from hearing the voice of God. The Bible says that God dwells with the humble (see Isaiah 57:15). This means that God's glory is among the humble. Pride will deny you access to the deep things of God. Once pride is removed, then will you be ready for a glory visitation.

During the life of Jesus, the Pharisees missed the move of God. They rejected the time of His visitation (see Luke 19:44). Being prideful and religious caused them to miss what God was doing. God is getting ready to do new things in the last days that we have never seen. This glory visitation is going to be supernatural, awesome, powerful, and exciting. Don't let pride cause you to miss this visitation.

In this last-day move of God, the spirit of evangelism will be restored. Thousands of souls will be saved. Whole families will come to Christ. Afflicted bodies will be healed. The atmosphere of heaven will invade earth. It's going to be like it was with Adam in the Garden of Eden. The supernatural was common to Adam. The supernatural is going to become common among the last day remnant. There will be a greater level of unity in the body of Christ amongst the remnant.

The sad thing is, like it was in the days of Jesus, there will be religious people who will miss the move of God. I remember having a vision where I saw people from all walks of life, bent over weeping in a large city. I was the only one in the city who was standing. I didn't know what was going on as I looked around, the city was full of people, weeping everywhere.

Then, I heard the voice of the spirit quote to me Romans 8:22, "For we know that the whole creation groaneth and travaileth in pain together until now." Then the revelation came to me, I was seeing a revival breakout. I believe I was witnessing a glory visitation. When the glory shows up, everyone becomes arrested by the by the Father's power.

I pray that this chapter encourages you to believe for God to give you a personal glory encounter.

CHAPTER 9

The Power of the Spoken Word

The centurion desired for Christ to come to his home to heal his servant that was sick and paralyzed. As Christ was on his way to heal this man's servant, he stopped Christ in his tracks. Feeling unworthy for the Messiah to come under his roof, he tells Christ, just speak the word. Christ in his astonishment says, I have not saw so great of faith, no not in Israel.

Why did Jesus marvel at this man's statement? Jesus marveled because he saw that this understood the power of the spoken word. Through that spoken word, the centurion's servant was healed in the same hour. I want to remind you was that we, too, have power in our words.

As we go back to the book of Genesis, the protology of all creation, we see that God *created* the heavens and the earth. *Created* originated from the Hebrew word *bara*, which means new, out of nothing, to bring into existence. God was so awesome that he took nothing, made something out of nothing, and that something was the earth.

In His infinite wisdom and creative ability, He speaks the world into existence. You too have that same creative inner dynamic to possess that divine nature on the inside which gives us supernatural abilities to speak our world and reality into existence. God speaks from His place of power and authority. He spoke this earth into existence for the Bible declares that by faith we understand that God framed the world by His word (see Hebrews 11:3). The Bible teaches us that which He spoke began to materialize.

In Genesis 1, the term "God said" is referenced 10 times. Then, the scriptures shift and say "God saw" 7 times. Therefore, God began to see what He had said. God wants us to begin to tap into the divine nature that exists on the inside of us, and when you begin to speak from that supernatural nature, then will you begin to see your words come into manifestation and materialize.

You have to be remain aware of the place at which you are speaking from. If you speak from the realm of flesh and carnality, nothing will begin to transpire. If you begin to speak from the realm of God, then will you see your words materializing and manifesting before your very eyes. God says in Isaiah 55:11, "the words that go forth out of my mouth shall not return unto me void, but it shall accomplish and that which I please and it shall prosper where to I have sent it."

This means when God speaks a word, that word will not return back onto God void. When God speaks a word, that word is full of power. God says when he speaks the word that he watches over that word to perform it (see Jeremiah 1:12). God is obligated to perform the very word in which He speaks, as well as what you speak through Him, because it is His word. God will always respond to His own word.

Whether that word is coming from God or whether that word is coming from you, and the Bible says that God confirmeth the word of his servant (See Isaiah 44:26). That means when you speak a word heaven, angels, and the Holy Spirit, the representative of God's power begins to back up that word by way of change, shifting, signs, wonders, and miracles. Jesus said, "The words that I speak unto you they are spirit, and they are life." (see John 6:63).

That word *life* comes from the Greek word *zoe* that means the word in which you speak, it has life. It's not an empty, lifeless word. That's why the word of God is so powerful because it is life and it is spirit. Jesus said that it is the spirit that is quickening thee. The word quicken means to make a life. There is life to that word. So, when you're speaking the word, you're speaking the living word that's why things begin to happen.

We see in Hebrews 4:12, "The word of God is quick and powerful". That word quick comes from the Greek word *zao* which means life. Then, he said *and powerful,* that word powerful comes from the Greek word *energes,* which means operative, effective, and active. So, not only is the word life, but the word of God is active. The word of God is quick, and powerful, and sharper than any two-edged sword, piercing even to the dividing asunder of soul and spirit, and of the joints and marrow, and is a discerner of the thoughts and intents of the heart."

The centurion understood the power of the spoken word. Once Christ speaks a word over you, that word becomes law. Once that word becomes law, that word becomes immutable which means that word cannot be changed, altered, or modified. The devil cannot countermand or dismantle that word because that word is law.

When you speak a word, speak from a kingly position (see Revelations 1:6). When you speak from a kingly position, that word in which you speak becomes law. The Bible says in the book of Job 22:28, "Thou shalt also decree a thing, and it shall be established unto thee". The word decree means to ordain, to establish, and to legislate by saying. Judges and kings have the power to decree. If you are a king, that means you too have the power to decree and speak from that place of authority and power.

What place are you speaking from? Are you speaking from a carnal place? Are you speaking from an immature place? Or are you speaking from a kingly place? Are you speaking from a heavenly place? Are you speaking from a God place? Are you speaking from a place of dominion, power, and authority?

The Bible teaches us how God has raised us up, and have made us to so sit together in heavenly places. This means that in the realm of the spirit, I am seated in heavenly realms. In the physical or the terrestrial realm, I'm still here on Earth. But, in the spiritual or in the eternal realm I am seated in heavenly places.

Because I am seated in heavenly places as a joint heir with Christ, I should be speaking from the place in which I am seated. When you begin to speak from that kingly place, or from that place in which you're seated in the heavenly realm, your words begin to move, change, and shift things. Because you're speaking with weight, you're speaking with power from God's realm.

Not from the realm of earth, but you're speaking from a heavenly place. That's why Jesus could speak the word and his words alone healed the centurion soldier because Jesus was not speaking from the earth realm, Jesus was speaking from the realm of heaven. He was speaking from the source of all power and that is God. When you speak from that realm, the God of that realm will cause things to begin to happen supernaturally.

When we look at Joshua, the Bible said then he commanded the sun to stand still which means that when he spoke from that realm, He affected the solar system (see Joshua 10:12). Can you imagine a mortal man quoting to the Scriptures commanding the sun the stand still? The reason why he was able to do that was because he was speaking from his divinity. When we look at Elijah the prophet, he opened his mouth during the time of famine, and he says, "there will be no rain nor do these years but according to my word" (see 1 Kings 17:1). That means that it did not rain for the space of 3 ½ years because of the words in which the prophet had spoken.

Do you know how that happened? It happened because he was speaking from his divinity. When I say your divinity, I'm talking about the God and the Jesus that lives in you. There was a divinity, there was a divine one, and there was a call that lived in Jesus. Colossians 1:19 says, "for it pleased the Father that in Jesus shall all of the fullness dwell." God dwelled in Him and because of that, when he spoke it was as if God himself was speaking.

When you speak the word of God, it is as if God or Jesus Himself is speaking. The Holy Spirit's responsibility and ministry is to undergird the word in which you speak by bringing that word to pass. When Elijah the prophet was being mocked by forty-two children, the Bible says that he commanded two she-bears to them (see 2 Kings 23:24).

When he tapped into his divinity, his authority, his words affected and influenced the animal kingdom. Two she-bears came out of nowhere in subjection to the authority of the prophets' words and mauled forty-two taunters.

That's power! The reason why it's important that you speak the word because the Bible declares that God is going to judge every idle word (see Matthew 12:36). *Idle* in the Greek *argos* means fruitless. Every word that you've been speaking that has not been producing positively, God says he's going to judge it.

He's going to judge every fruitless word, every word that's not producing kingdom, righteousness, holiness, or God. When you speak a word, angels are given the assignment to bring that word to pass. The Bible says, "Blessed is the Lord ye his angels that excelled in strength that do His commandments hearkening to the voice of his word..." (see Psalm 103:20). Angels hearken to the voice of God.

There are angels right now that are standing in Heaven as if they are unemployed because the saints here on earth will not give them assignments by the spoken word. They will not respond to words of flesh, but when you speak the word of God, according to Psalms, "they will hasten to that word to perform it." (see Jeremiah 1:12).

This is the season to begin to give your angels assignments by speaking the word. As you speak the word, whether it's a word of deliverance, of breakthrough, a financial word, a word of prosperity, or a word of faith, angels are assigned to bring that word to pass. When the preacher is preaching at church, the reason why they have saints that leave without receiving anything in the realm of the spirit is simple. It's because there are people that come to church who not connect with that word with faith and expectation.

When you're putting a demand on the preacher's anointing, with faith and expectation, angels are then sent to that sanctuary to begin to materialize that word in your life. That's why it is good to connect with that word in faith or by sowing into that word because you give the angels, the theophanic beings, and access to begin to perform that very word in your life. It is time to begin to speak the word, to decree, to declare, and legislate.

Decree means to legislate by saying, to order, to command, to give a charge or directive. But to declare in Hebrew or in Greek means 'to make known'. So, when you decree, you're legislating by saying, and when you declare you are making known what you decreed. The Lord is saying that this is the season for you to arise and to begin to decree, and to declare.

Begin to speak peace, joy, power, deliverance, health, miracles, signs, wonders, and breakthrough. Some of you have allowed the devil to begin to muzzle your mouth from speaking your world into existence. Didn't I tell you that you and I have been created in the very image and likeness of God?

We were created to be the visible representation of God in the earth. So, we're to imitate God in the earth. As God has spoken the world into existence, we too are called to speak our world into existence. Remember when God had created the heavens, and the earth, God then, "forms man out of the dust and he breathes into man the breath of man becomes a living soul" (Genesis 2:7).

God as king rules the heaven and God created man to be king over the earth. The Bible says that God brought the animals unto Adam to see what he would name them. Adam lived in the supernatural, Adam breathed the supernatural, Adam was the supernatural, and he lived in the glory in the supernatural. When you're speaking from a place of glory things will begin to happen. Things will begin to shake and to move.

You have a God that lives in you. Stop allowing yourself to be defeated by the adversary that is sent against your life that's been sent to muzzle your mouth and stop your every word. You've got to begin to speak your reality into existence. That means tomorrow morning get up and begin to decree, to declare, to speak to your world into existence. Everything that you need, remember, Jesus said, "the Kingdom of God cometh not by way of observation." He said, "But the kingdom of God that is within *me*..." (Luke 17:20-21).

Speak from your kingdom place. Everything that you need is locked and concealed inside of your kingdom and you must begin to pull out of your kingdom the very thing in which you need. The way you do that is by beginning to speak out of your mouth what's locked in your kingdom.

Your mouth is the gateway for everything that's in your kingdom to come out of, but Satan has sent his demonic agents as guards to guard the gate of your mouth from speaking what God has commanded you to speak. What are you speaking in this season?

God spoke to me years ago and said Dave, the Earth has an ear. He said when you take the 'th' off the word earth, you have 'ear'. God declares in the book of Jeremiah, God says, "Oh earth, oh earth, oh earth hear the word of the Lord..." (see Jeremiah 22:29).

Throughout the Scripture, the earth has always been given a female gender. The Bible always called earth a 'her', which means she has conceiving ability. The earth can get pregnant, but what is she looking to conceive? She's looking to conceive the seeds of the spoken word.

The Bible calls the Word of God the engrafted Word of God. The word engrafted in the Greek, *emphutos* means implanted. The Word of God is the seed Christ was speaking. In one of His parables in which He was speaking, Jesus identified the Word of

God as a seed. So, the earth has conceiving
potential, but she's waiting on you and me to
begin to speak the word as seed into her.
Once she conceives the word as seed, she
can begin to produce the harvest of that seed.

The assignment of the earth has always been
to yield forth your fruit and harvest. Do you
not know that the earth was created to obey
you? The earth was created to submit to you.
This earth was created to be subject to you.

That's why we have farmers. The farmer
understands agriculture and begins to
cultivate, or till the soil. There's nothing the
soil could do about it, but to receive the seed,
go through the process that the farmer has
taken her through, and yield that farmers
harvest.

When will you rise up and begin to operate
in your divinity as a godly man and as a godly
woman? Will you take charge and speak?
Will you operate in your kingly anointing?
Did not Paul say in Ephesians 5:1, "Beloved,

be there for the followers of God as dear children." Followers, in the Greek *mimetes,* means imitator. We were called to imitate God as kingdom ambassadors, ecclesiastical leaders, and apostolic, prophetic and evangelistic agents.

We have been called to duplicate everything that God does in earth. That's why when Philip asked Jesus the question, "Jesus show us the Father?" Jesus responds, "Phillip you mean to tell me all this time you've been with me you still have not seen the Father? Jesus said, "If you have seen me, you have seen the Father." Jesus said, "The words that I speak, I speak them of my Father." (see John 14:6-14).

Everything that Jesus did, He tried to do it just like his daddy, God. Everything that God did in the scriptures, you're called to emulate. Some of you may feel like you don't know if you can operate in that level of power. Absolutely, you can! The Bible said that Jesus had the Spirit without measure.

Did not the Bible call you a joint heir with Christ? That means to operate in that realm, or in that dimension, that is your inheritance as the son or daughter of the living God.

To begin to speak with power, to begin to decree and to declare, that is your God-given ability. Do you not know as a Kingdom citizen, those are all parts of your benefits and God-given inheritance? Stop living your life in defeat and begin to take authority over your mouth and begin to speak like your daddy God.

Begin to speak like Adam did in the Garden of Eden as God brought the animals unto Adam to see what he would name them (See Genesis 2:20). Don't you dare allow the enemy to stop you from opening up your mouth speaking your reality into existence. Begin to prophesy the word of the Lord. It is time to begin to speak for the word of the Lord. The Word of God is powerful, the Word of God has life. *Word* translates in Hebrew to *dawbaw,* which means power, promise, purpose, provision, protection, and prophetic revelation.

Once you've spoken that word, you then must begin to hold on to that word. Don't you dare allow that adversary to cause you to abort or miscarry your baby. No more spiritual stillborn babies! Hold, guard, and preserve your baby. Now as a glory carrier speak the word with power in your generation.

I pray that after reading this book that the glory realm becomes unlocked to you. I pray that you receive spiritual impartation and activation. I pray that a supernatural grace comes upon you to apply the principals of fasting, prayer and consecration that's mentioned in this book.

Lord, help the reader to develop a lifestyle of self-discipline to maintain access to the glory realm. Now, I encourage you to get ready to enter and experience a greater realm of glory.

ABOUT THE AUTHOR

Prophet David Alan Taylor is a sought-after revivalist, prophetic voice and apostolic leader with a message of consecration and prayer. Taylor produces monthly program on 101.5 FM called "The Keys to the Kingdom Broadcast," which reaches 2 million people in Houston and surrounding areas. Taylor is also the creator and master teacher of *The Prophet's Lab* where he educates and equips God's prophets. Taylor also pastors the Glory Center in Houston, TX.

Prophet Taylor was born in Springfield, Illinois with 4 brothers and sisters. Growing up in an unchurched, two parent household, Taylor began seeing demons and having supernatural experiences as early as age 5. Exposed to church at the age of 11 years old by his grandmother, Taylor had no clue that the call of God was on his life. As a teenager, Taylor lived a sinful life as a drug dealer although multiple demonic encounters continued.

It was at 17 years old that Taylor was exposed to the Holy Spirit after an invited to church by a friend and gave his life to Jesus. Under the Leadership of Pastor C.C. Doss, he developed a hunger for prayer and consecration. At age

18, Taylor mounted the pulpit to begin to proclaim the Word of God. Years later, under the leadership of Apostle Melvin Brown of Rockford, Illinois, Prophet Taylor was trained not only in the scriptures, but in the importance of studying and effectively communicating a text.

During this tenure of sonship, Taylor began operating heavily in the prophetic gift. Accurate words of knowledge, personal prophecy, prophetic dreams and the spirit of revelation were developed under this ministry. Taylor traveled the state for years as a revivalist, proclaiming and prophesying to the people of God as well as the unsaved who God would lead him to minister to.

Prophet Taylor moved to the city of Houston in 2012 and began a successful church in Spring, TX. He desires to preach the message of Christ on all 7 continents and believes that the prophetic ministry, and most importantly the word of God, is essential in this dispensation of time. Prophet Taylor and his wife Randryia reside in Houston, TX.

For more information about Prophet David Alan Taylor, or to contact the author for speaking engagements visit www.theprophetslab.com